Real Estate
and North Carolina Law

A RESIDENT'S PRIMER

Charles Szypszak

2012

UNC
SCHOOL OF
GOVERNMENT

The School of Government at the University of North Carolina at Chapel Hill works to improve the lives of North Carolinians by engaging in practical scholarship that helps public officials and citizens understand and improve state and local government. Established in 1931 as the Institute of Government, the School provides educational, advisory, and research services for state and local governments. The School of Government is also home to a nationally ranked graduate program in public administration and specialized centers focused on information technology and environmental finance.

As the largest university-based local government training, advisory, and research organization in the United States, the School of Government offers up to 200 courses, webinars, and specialized conferences for more than 12,000 public officials each year. In addition, faculty members annually publish approximately fifty books, book chapters, bulletins, and other reference works related to state and local government. Each day that the General Assembly is in session, the School produces the *Daily Bulletin*, which reports on the day's activities for members of the legislature and others who need to follow the course of legislation.

The Master of Public Administration Program is a full-time, two-year program that serves up to sixty students annually. It consistently ranks among the best public administration graduate programs in the country, particularly in city management. With courses ranging from public policy analysis to ethics and management, the program educates leaders for local, state, and federal governments and nonprofit organizations.

Operating support for the School of Government's programs and activities comes from many sources, including state appropriations, local government membership dues, private contributions, publication sales, course fees, and service contracts. Visit www.sog.unc.edu or call 919.966.5381 for more information on the School's courses, publications, programs, and services.

Michael R. Smith, DEAN
Thomas H. Thornburg, SENIOR ASSOCIATE DEAN
Frayda S. Bluestein, ASSOCIATE DEAN FOR FACULTY DEVELOPMENT
Todd A. Nicolet, ASSOCIATE DEAN FOR OPERATIONS
Ann Cary Simpson, ASSOCIATE DEAN FOR DEVELOPMENT
Bradley G. Volk, ASSOCIATE DEAN FOR ADMINISTRATION

FACULTY

Gregory S. Allison
David N. Ammons
Ann M. Anderson
A. Fleming Bell, II
Maureen M. Berner
Mark F. Botts
Michael Crowell
Shea Riggsbee Denning
James C. Drennan
Richard D. Ducker
Joseph S. Ferrell
Alyson A. Grine
Norma Houston
Cheryl Daniels Howell
Jeffrey A. Hughes

Willow S. Jacobson
Robert P. Joyce
Kenneth L. Joyner
Diane M. Juffras
Dona G. Lewandowski
James M. Markham
Janet Mason
Christopher B. McLaughlin
Laurie L. Mesibov
Kara A. Millonzi
Jill D. Moore
Jonathan Q. Morgan
Ricardo S. Morse
C. Tyler Mulligan
David W. Owens

William C. Rivenbark
Dale J. Roenigk
John Rubin
Jessica Smith
Karl W. Smith
Carl W. Stenberg III
John B. Stephens
Charles Szypszak
Shannon H. Tufts
Vaughn Upshaw
Aimee N. Wall
Jeffrey B. Welty
Richard B. Whisnant
Gordon P. Whitaker

Contents

Dedication

The law is an expression of our will. Does our law speak of intelligent commitment to liberty and justice? As a human design, law can represent collective achievement or weakness. Self-satisfaction and envy are facets of human frailty that pave the way for the destructive tyranny of despots and crowds alike. This book is dedicated to those who want to live peaceably with their neighbors and enjoy the fruits of their honest labor, and who insist that the law bring honor to our capacity for respecting individual rights and responsibilities.

Introduction

We depend on real estate law for roofs over our heads and food on our tables. We depend on it to run businesses and save for retirement. Its fundamental importance is obvious, but its details are not. We may all have an instinctive sense about private property rights, but few know much about the laws that enable us to own and transfer real estate. We usually need not worry about this reality. We assume we will be protected by lawyers and real estate professionals whom we engage to represent our interests. Fortunately this assumption usually turns out to be correct, and we rarely need to struggle to understand the finer points of real estate law. Yet whether out of general curiosity, or focused concern about protecting rights and interests, we can benefit from a better understanding of the basic laws and procedures that affect real estate ownership and transfer.

The information in this book is based on the author's decades of experience as a practicing lawyer and advisor to public officials. It includes answers to many of the questions that are often asked by real estate purchasers and owners, public officials, and others who deal with real estate. Topics are arranged in four chapters that pertain to the main aspects of real estate ownership and transfer. Chapter 1 addresses fundamental concepts of private property ownership and the restrictions on it, including such things as land use restrictions, roads, eminent domain, and taxes. Chapter 2 contains basic information about how real estate is owned, including such things as co-ownership arrangements, and shared real estate interests, such as easements, leases, and condominiums. Chapter 3 addresses the main aspects of real estate transfers, including contracts and purchase closings, and the roles of the main players in that process, including brokers and lawyers. Chapter 4 addresses real estate financing, including basic information about loans, deeds of trust, and foreclosures. The table of contents and index provide links to the many specific topics contained within these chapters.

This book is intended as an introduction to the basics of real estate law in North Carolina for someone who does not have a legal education but who wants to know more about the subject. It is not a substitute for legal representation or advice, and it is not by itself a sufficient resource for making decisions about real estate purchases or loans or the resolution of disputes. Like many other fields that involve an array of interrelated issues and competing considerations, real estate law is constantly evolving. One of the challenges of the law is just to know what statutes, rules, or principles may be implicated. Fully understanding the law requires extensive law training and experience. This book can only be a frame around a very complicated picture. But it can be helpful for understanding basic real estate law better and appreciating the need for expert advice and representation when appropriate.

1 Property Rights and Restrictions

This chapter introduces the basics of the law governing real estate ownership and transfer in North Carolina. These basics include private property rights and the restrictions and obligations that go along with them, including land use regulations, eminent domain power to take private property for public use, public road access, and real estate taxes.

1.1 Land as Property

North Carolina comprises roughly thirty-one million acres of land. The federal government holds about fourteen percent of that land for such public purposes as protected forests, park lands, and military bases. Another one-half percent is held by state and local government for public purposes. About fifty-six thousand acres are tribal and local lands.[1] The rest of the land in the state—the vast majority of it—is privately owned. Despite sprawling urban areas, large industrial zones, expanding commercial uses, and burgeoning residential communities, the majority of this privately owned land remains rural and undeveloped. The North Carolina landscape is still being drawn, and the laws that govern it are still taking shape.

Most Americans share a general sense of what it means to own real estate. This may stem from the notion of a home as a sanctuary and valuable asset that can be sold or left to someone by will. The notion may be simple, but the law of real estate ownership and transfer is complex, and the details can be surprising. It has evolved over the centuries, originating with imported English law and constantly molded into modern shape as courts have resolved disputes and legislatures have passed laws to address changing conditions. Much has changed as the country has grown and competition for land has intensified. But still at the core of real estate law are the same basic principles that were recognized in the early republic about individual rights to acquire, develop, and transfer property. Understanding this law involves looking into both long-standing legal traditions and modern legislative solutions.

North Carolina is among the richest natural areas, with seacoast, mountains, and vast stretches of land. Real estate law first took shape in this state when there was plenty of open space. Settlers relied on laws to protect their claims and build their communities. Neighbors rarely had to worry about exactly where a boundary was, and public officials did not have to deal with highways, industrial pollution, and public transportation systems. Despite the rarity of conflicts, the predictability of law was important.

Real estate law became much more complicated as the competition for land increased. As the adage goes, land is something that cannot be manufactured, and demands on it have intensified with population growth and the arrival of modern industry and transportation systems. What

---

1. Natural Resources Council of Maine, Public Land Ownership by State (table based on data compiled in 1995 by the National Wilderness Institute), *available at* www.nrcm.org/documents/publiclandownership.pdf.

was once a hundred-acre tract governed by basic ownership notions may now be a subdivision with scores of homes, shared sewer and water systems and roads, and recreational amenities subject to specialized laws and multilayered development restrictions and association agreements. The laws that now govern real estate involve such diverse rules and concepts as condominium regimes, environmental regulations, subdivision covenants, and intertwined local, state, and federal eminent domain powers and procedures.

The starting point for making sense of law in this field is to appreciate what is considered to be "real estate" or "real property," because whatever fits this definition is subject to a special body of laws. There are many other kinds of property that can be possessed and to which enforceable legal rights can exist, including such things as contracts and inventions. This book is concerned only with real estate, which includes land and structures and other permanent improvements made upon land, such as homes, apartment buildings, farms, stores, factories, roads, and sewer and water systems. Real estate also includes trees and other natural growth, and minerals in the ground, although these kinds of things can be removed and sold just like other non–real estate property. Traditionally standing timber also has been considered to be real estate, but under the modern code that governs most commercial sale transactions it is treated as non–real estate when it is subject to a contract for sale. Crops while growing are part of the real estate, but because they are harvested and sold as commodities they also are subject to many of the rules that apply to other kinds of commercial goods.

The notion of what constitutes real estate is further complicated by the fact that things can be real estate at certain times but not at others. For example, a fixture, such as a lighting device or appliance that will become part of a building, is not real estate when it is shipped from the store, but it becomes real estate when it is permanently installed in a building. Another type of property that has both real estate and non–real estate characteristics is a manufactured home, which the law defines as a transportable structure that can be installed on a permanent foundation.[2] Such a structure is often placed on leased land in cluster arrangements, and because it is similar to other types of real estate it is subject to many of the same laws. But it also is subject to specialized laws because it has some unique

---

2. Section 143-145(7) of the North Carolina General Statutes (hereinafter G.S.).

characteristics. Among these laws are statutes that prohibit local governments from adopting zoning regulations that have the effect of excluding manufactured homes from the entire jurisdiction.[3] However, cities and counties may adopt requirements for manufactured homes. These do not affect what are known as modular homes, which are built in a factory but meet the same general construction standards of the state building code as apply to site-built homes. Special legal considerations also apply to the transfer of these kinds of property and how such things as deeds of trust apply to them.

Whether a traditional home, installed fixture, land product, or transportable building, property that is considered to be real estate under the law is subject to legal principles that fundamentally have remained the same for centuries but that have evolved in response to changing conditions. This book addresses many of these laws.

1.2 Constitutional Rights

Private property rights are among the most fundamental notions in American legal culture. They are at the foundation of homeownership and the market economy. Many people are naturally surprised that a notion so well accepted as private property is not mentioned in the Declaration of Independence or the United States or North Carolina constitutions. This lack of mention has not been interpreted by courts as raising doubt about the right; instead, it has been seen as reflecting how the framers accepted it as so embedded in liberty and individual rights that it did not need to be separately declared.

Although the U.S. Constitution does not mention a right to property ownership in such words, the Fifth Amendment implicitly recognizes it when it prohibits the government from taking private property for public use without just compensation. The North Carolina courts have made clear that property rights are implicitly fundamental under the N.C. Constitution as well. Although the state constitution does not directly speak of a right of private property, it acknowledges this right when it prohibits state government deprivation of private property "but by the law of the

---

3. G.S. 153A-341.1; G.S. 160A-383.1.

land" and for just compensation. If the government must follow due process and pay for taking it, then the right to it must exist.

The concept of a *right of private property* that these constitutional principles reflect suggests possessing something that need not be shared with others. This is the legal notion of *exclusivity*, which is an owner's right to prevent others from using private property without permission. Rights of exclusivity preserve the owner's ability to enjoy the essential benefits of real estate ownership, but owners can share these rights, as they do in co-ownership arrangements, as discussed in Section 2.1, and when limited rights are given to neighbors as easements, as discussed in Section 2.3. The private ownership concept also entails an expectation of a right to sell, to use it as collateral for a loan, and to leave it to someone after death. This set of rights is known as *alienability*. When courts consider cases involving real estate they often invoke the principles of exclusivity and alienability without mentioning them by name.

Exclusivity and alienability are not absolute. They are affected by the government's powers to protect the interests of the community. Government power over private property has always existed, but its application has expanded as use of land has become more congested and potentially toxic uses have proliferated. Changes in the law are not surprising given how much conditions have evolved. When the U.S. Constitution was first ratified more than 220 years ago, and federal and state laws were first enacted based on its framework, the United States had fewer than three million people, only a small percentage of whom owned land. Under the conditions in the late 1700s when the American legal system was framed, boundaries between ownership were far apart. As an example of how differently people may have looked at their property rights, when the government took land to build roads in the early Republic, landowners welcomed the action and did not expect compensation. Roads connected their land to transportation networks and made vacant areas more usable. Today, governments often face resistance by real estate owners when congested roads are expanded, and disagreements commonly arise about the economic impact of the project and owners' expectations about compensation as a result of it.

Despite these changes, modern law still basically protects private rights to exclude others from real estate and to transfer it. The most fundamental change in the reach of the law is in restrictions on how land can be used. One owner's use is now more likely to have an impact on another's. Careful planning is needed for some kinds of modern industrial and commercial uses to coexist with home sites and natural preserves. So the courts and legislatures necessarily have had to reconcile competing claims of rights with legitimate concerns about impact, and the details of the real estate laws have become more complex. While the notion of private property still is at the core of the law, many aspects of ownership now entail restrictions and obligations. There are many federal and state environmental laws and regulations prohibiting or restricting uses that can pollute the air or water. The courts have upheld these laws as legitimate uses of the government's inherent police power, requiring compensation only in extreme circumstances. Some of these circumstances are discussed later in this chapter.

Modern real estate ownership usually involves many other kinds of laws for which there was no need when the legal system was first established. For example, homeownership now usually involves institutional financing, and commercial development often entails complex financial structures. Most who borrow money for real estate purchases have no experience that enables them to understand the details of loan payments or lender foreclosure rights, and even sophisticated developers can be mystified by the intricacies of commercial loans. Federal and state law now imposes many requirements on lending practices. These rules aim at ensuring that lenders inform borrowers about their financing choices and the obligations to which they will be agreeing by mandating disclosures at various stages of the loan-making process. Legislatures have reacted to recent trouble in the mortgage markets with additional restrictions on lending and foreclosure. These lending laws are constantly being refined.

Despite the law's expanding breadth and complexity and the increasing influence of complicated federal laws and regulations, the same basic laws have always governed real estate ownership. These are state laws. Although they are essentially the same in all of the states, the details of them can vary, sometimes in important ways. Even the most basic legal terminology can mean different things in different states. North Carolina law is mostly similar to the law in other states, including the basic nature of rights to own and to convey, but the description of North Carolina law in this book should not be assumed to be the same in any other state.

The laws discussed in this book are a framework on which all real estate transactions must be built. Despite the importance of understanding the law, real estate ownership and transfer in the United States is still largely a matter of individual choices. Unlike in some countries, in the United States the government does not regulate or confirm real estate ownership transfers. The government regulates but does not dictate boundaries, and it plays no role in setting prices for real estate transfer. This is in stark contrast to the legal regimes in many other countries in which a government office reviews and approves transfers. Here sellers, buyers, and lenders are mostly left to their own means of determining what rights can be conveyed, documenting the conveyance, and protecting themselves against loss. The government only provides the parties to a transaction with a method for making a public record of their transfers. This means real estate owners must rely on lawyers and other professionals to protect their interests when they purchase real estate or arrange financing. A basic understanding of real estate law and the manner in which it can be transferred does not replace the need for this advice. It is a foundation for better informed choices.

1.3 Land Use Controls

Extensive regulation of land use began early in the twentieth century to try to address problems with haphazard growth and dangers of intermingled industrial, commercial, agricultural, and residential uses. The courts generally have upheld the constitutionality of restrictions as long as they bear a rational relationship to the community's health and safety. Rational regulations are based on analysis of many factors, including existing real estate uses, environmental conditions, and growth patterns. Their restrictiveness can rationally increase as land uses become more crowded.

Legislatures have adopted many statutes aimed at coordinating new construction to address environmental concerns and to encourage development patterns perceived as desirable. Their effect does not always match the expectations of owners or their neighbors. Individual landowners tend to view their investment in real estate as empowering them to make their own reasonable choices about its development and sale. In practice these competing concerns about protection and fair use are worked out in an uncomfortable compromise. Some rules about development are clear—certain uses are allowed only in certain areas. This can be determined by examining the applicable zoning ordinance and zoning maps. But land use control is not a system of clearly defined rules about what landowners can and cannot do. Often the ability to use real estate in a certain way is a matter of how local government officials and neighbors view the proposal.

Most of the time an owner's use of real estate fits with the land use regulations, either as an initial design or after compromise in the approval process. When dispute arises a resolution is available in court, but the courts tend to be more concerned about whether the rules were applied consistently, and the prescribed procedure followed, than with the merits of the development proposal. Judges often note that they will not overturn a land use regulatory decision just because they would have reached a different result. And even when courts do find the outcome of a particular decision to be unreasonable, the usual result is to send the matter back to the same officials who reached the unreasonable result, leaving the owner to another process of uncertain outcome with officials who are now even less favorably disposed to support the owner's position.

1.3.1 Police Power

Among the restrictions on private real estate is the government's *police power* to protect public health, safety, and general welfare. This regulatory power has always been part of American law. The sweeping terms used to describe it become meaningful only within the context of particular circumstances, such as the laws of nuisance or permissible zoning restrictions. The North Carolina General Assembly invokes this authority when it gives to counties and municipalities the power to "define, prohibit, regulate, or abate acts, omissions, or conditions, detrimental to the health, safety, or welfare of its citizens and the peace and dignity of the city."[4] These are general terms within which many laws can be justified, but the government is required to exercise this power in a reasonable manner and degree. Courts generally defer to legislatures to make these determinations, but they will invalidate restrictions on private land use that are obviously unreasonable or arbitrary. There are many cases in which landowners have successfully challenged a particular interpretation of a regulation because it was incorrectly or unreasonably applied under the particular circumstances, but courts rarely strike down the restriction as invalid.

The police power may be used to restrict private property uses in general to protect public health and safety, even if it makes affected real estate less valuable than it otherwise might be or become. This recognizes the fact that all changes in the law governing development have some effect on market values—market values are based on the highest and best possible use of the real estate given its characteristics, including its access to public facilities, the kinds of other properties in the neighborhood, and what by

---

4. G.S. 160A-174 (municipalities); G.S. 153A-121 (counties).

law is allowed to be built. Whatever the economic logic, any system of land regulation would be unwieldy if an attempt were made to require all landowners affected by a regulation to be paid from publicly raised revenues or if government attempted to recover all windfalls to owners caused by government action.

In general, the courts have expanded the notion of permissible regulations as local governments have perceived more need to address harm from industry and crowding. But on rare occasions they have warned that compensation to an owner may be required if a regulation is excessively restrictive. According to famous words of the U.S. Supreme Court, "The general rule at least, is that while property may be regulated to a certain extent, if regulation goes too far it will be recognized as a taking" by the government for which compensation must be paid.[5] A difficult question with which owners and courts have struggled is when any particular regulation "goes too far." All land use regulations affect real estate values to some degree, and the courts have rejected the proposition that owners are entitled to compensation for every diminution in real estate value resulting from a restriction. But in rare circumstances a regulation has been found to be invalid because it rendered particularly valuable real estate virtually useless.

1.3.2 Environmental Laws

There are many environmental laws at all three levels of government: federal, state, and local. They are particularly detailed for land uses that produce waste or pollutants. Such uses usually are prohibited unless a permit is first obtained from an agency, such as the U.S. Environmental Protection Agency (EPA), that ensures compliance with limits on the amount and handling of discharges. Federal laws also restrict uses of real estate in sensitive areas, such as a waterways and wetlands, and if they will have a major impact on natural resources, such as mining. Federal laws require environmental assessments and impact statements for major projects permitted or funded by federal agencies, such as airports and highways. Federal law also allocates responsibility for cleanup of hazardous waste sites and gives agencies authority to recover costs from responsible parties. This is known as the *Superfund law*, and its application has resulted in large-scale projects

---

5. Pennsylvania Coal Co. v. Mahon, 260 U.S. 393, 415 (1922).

to remedy environmental contamination at industrial sites throughout the country.

The EPA often coordinates its activities through state environmental protection agencies. North Carolina statutes contain their own restrictions on development and discharges into the land, water, and air within the state. They also aim at protecting statewide resources, such as watersheds and coastal areas. Any development that will have an impact on these resources is likely to be subject to an extensive review and permitting process governed by federal and state statutes. The preparation of permit applications and responses to regulator concerns usually requires the expertise of engineers and professional consultants who have experience with the process, such as those who work with environmental consulting firms.

1.3.3 Building Codes

The most detailed regulations that apply to buildings are *building codes*, which throughout the country have many common features. Building codes are intended to ensure safe construction. Most people do not have the knowledge or means of checking for such things as foundation soundness, safe electrical wiring, and materials and construction that minimize the risk of fire. Building codes are designed to address these matters.

The North Carolina State Building Code applies throughout the state and is enforced by city and county inspectors. It is based on a national standard with extensive and detailed specifications for overall building design, construction dimensions and materials, mechanical systems, plumbing and electrical, and many other aspects. The code is enforced by a requirement that someone first obtain a permit before construction or major changes. The permit can be obtained only if the applicant can show that the work will comply with the code. Compliance is then enforced with a requirement that the permit holder return for a certificate of occupancy before the building can be used, which is issued only after an inspection. Obtaining permits and occupancy certificates requires submission of detailed plans to code enforcement officers and the payment of fees based on the nature of the structure and the kind of work being performed. This permitting process is a source of revenue for local government, particularly to fund the inspection process.

1.3.4 Zoning and Planning Restrictions

Land use regulation in North Carolina is governed by state statutes that delegate authority to counties and municipalities to enact regulations and review and approve applications. State law establishes the basic permissible components of local land use regulation and the process for applying the rules to proposed construction. But local governments have considerable discretion to tailor their regulations to local conditions, and those who review applications for compliance have significant leeway in how the regulations are to be applied. Someone who conveys real estate that subdivides a parcel of record or builds without required approvals may be prosecuted for a criminal misdemeanor, and a court may order the owner to re-convey the real estate or otherwise to take action to correct the violation.[6]

The details of a land use regulation begin with the legislative body—council or commissioners—that adopts or amends ordinances that have the effect of laws. A public hearing must be held before an ordinance can be adopted. Local governments have *planning boards* to review proposed zoning ordinances and amendments to them.[7] Zoning ordinances regulate the location of real estate uses by designating areas for various general categories of commercial, industrial, residential, agricultural, and other uses. They also regulate building dimensions, lot sizes, building placement, and densities. Subdivision ordinances typically require that any division of land into smaller parts be approved, and the board that reviews the application considers proposed street access, drainage, water and sewage facilities, and other use features. Local governments have *zoning boards of adjustment* to hear appeals from administrative decisions, such as the denial of a building permit because the use is not allowed.[8] If no use issue is raised, most local governments require subdivisions to be approved by the planning board, though final approval of subdivision plats may be granted by governing boards or other designated bodies. The approval procedure usually requires submission of plans and includes public hearings at which neighbors have an opportunity to protest the proposal. Often a developer is required to make improvements to roads or to dedicate land for public use as part of an approval, especially for major projects, as well as to provide assurances of performance that improvements will be completed,

---

6. G.S. 153A-123; G.S. 153A-324; G.S. 153A-334(a); G.S. 160A-175; G.S. 160A-365; G.S. 160A-375.
7. G.S. 153A-344; G.S. 160A-387.
8. G.S. 153A-345; G.S. 160A-388.

such as a letter of credit or bond that could be used to finish promised subdivision roads.

For some communities the General Assembly has authorized local governments to regulate land uses beyond their territorial boundaries, something known as *extraterritorial jurisdiction*. This is intended to address land uses that do not originate within the jurisdiction but that have an impact on it, such as a discharge into a river that runs into the jurisdiction.

Zoning has traditionally been aimed at organizing neighborhoods, not at making individual decisions about what is appropriate on a particular lot. Zoning that singles out a particular tract can be challenged as unlawful *spot zoning*. A particular lot can be treated differently from others if there is a reasonable basis for it in view of adjacent land uses and the comprehensive plan, but it cannot be the result of favoritism or another basis not connected to the legitimate goals of zoning. As the N.C. Supreme Court explained, "[f]actors relevant to the reasonableness inquiry include, but are not necessarily limited to, the size of the tract in question; the compatibility of the disputed zoning action with an existing zoning plan; the benefits and detriments resulting from the zoning for the owner of the parcel, his neighbors, and the surrounding community; and the relationship between the uses envisioned under the new zoning and the uses currently present in the adjacent tracts."[9]

Subdivisions include large-scale developments of single family homes as well as splitting off a piece of one lot and adding it to a neighbor's. In North Carolina, several kinds of lot configuration changes are not considered subdivisions that are subject to the subdivision regulations. The exceptions to subdivision approval requirements include combining lots if the result does not increase the total number of lots and each of the created lots meet local minimum dimensional requirements, such as setbacks from lot lines; dividing land into parcels larger than ten acres if there is no street dedication involved; and dividing a lot of no greater than two acres into not more than three lots if the resulting lots comply with the standards and no street dedication is involved; or when the government takes a strip of land for public road widening.[10] When in doubt landowners should consult with local administrators to ensure that approval is not required.

---

9. Good Neighbors of S. Davidson v. Town of Denton, 355 N.C. 254, 258, 559 S.E.2d 768, 771 (2002).

10. G.S. 153A-335; G.S. 160A-376.

Communities use zoning to try to organize development in a way that will situate land uses to protect against harmful interference and facilitate the provision of public services. In theory, zoning is a master plan to guide growth rationally in ways that regulators presume will not occur naturally. Among the challenges to achieving this goal is the reality that the restrictions necessarily are based on what already exists in an area and that they protect already predominant uses, but the demand for land is driven by unpredictable market forces. Also, what may seem rational from a planner's perspective may seem arbitrary from an individual landowner's perspective. For example, while zoning may logically be used to attempt to draw a line between areas in which industrial and residential uses will be permitted, someone still will have real estate where these two zones meet and not enjoy the full advantage of a protected enclave for a single use. Many of the legal disputes that arise about zoning decisions involve owners who think the zoning map has arbitrarily impeded real estate development when viewed from that particular owner's perspective.

1.3.5 Zoning and Planning Procedures

If proposed construction is for a use that is among those listed in the zoning ordinance as *permitted by right* in the zone in which it is located, the zoning administrator may issue a permit without any need for a hearing on the proposed use. If the proposed construction is for a use that is allowed within the zone only as a *conditional use, special use*, or by *special exception*, the owner must submit an application to a board to show that certain conditions are satisfied. Typically such conditions include a review of the size of the proposed construction and its impact on the roads and neighboring parcels. Often the process results in minor changes in the specifics of the improvement configuration.

If a use is neither allowed by right nor by satisfying special standards, the owner can only construct for the use with a *variance*. A variance is a rarely available safety valve to protect owners from a zoning ordinance that may deprive the owner of *any* reasonable use. In most North Carolina municipalities and counties, the zoning board of adjustment has responsibility for considering requests for variances and may grant them only when specific state law conditions are met. A state statute provides as follows: "When practical difficulties or unnecessary hardships would result from carrying out the strict letter of a zoning ordinance, the board of adjustment shall have the power to vary or modify any of the regulations or provisions of the ordinance so that the spirit of the ordinance shall be observed, public safety and welfare secured, and substantial justice done."[11] A hardship for which a variance may be granted must have to do with the real estate configuration and how the variance peculiarly affects it—not the owner's financial circumstances or market conditions that make a particular use more valuable. The statute prohibits local governments from granting a variance to allow a use not authorized by the ordinance.[12]

The land use approval process varies in detail from jurisdiction to jurisdiction, but they all have common basic characteristics. In most cities and counties, zoning involves the governing board, planning board, zoning board of adjustment, and planning and zoning staff. The subdivision plat approval process applies primarily to single-family residential developments. Most local governments request an informal plan to be presented to the planning staff for comment. The formal process is then begun with a preliminary plat that shows the layout of the proposal, and it is on this plat that the staff provide their comments about compliance and what changes may be required for approval. Many jurisdictions have a different level of review for major and minor subdivisions based on the number of lots involved, with major subdivisions involving additional review steps and consultations. Public hearings are required for variances, conditional use permits, and appeals from a zoning official's decision. The hearings have both legislative and judicial aspects. Witnesses must be sworn and offer testimony according to certain rules of evidence, board members make written findings of fact, and a record is made of the decision and its basis. Once a final plat is approved it is signed by the governing authority and recorded in the county register of deeds' office before lots may be sold.

An owner who is denied an approval or permit, or someone who can point to special damages as a result of a board's decision, may appeal the decision to the superior court. In general the deadline for filing an appeal is thirty days, but anyone considering an appeal should be careful to find out the precise deadline for the particular matter. Failure to meet the deadline probably means no appeal can be filed. Only matters that involve discretion may be appealed, such as determinations about whether the standards have been met for variances and conditional use permits, and appeals from administrative decisions.[13] In general the court will rely

---

11. G.S. 153A-345(d); G.S. 160A-388(d).
12. *Id.*
13. G.S. 153A-349; G.S. 160A-393.

entirely on what was submitted to the board and a record of what was said at the hearing. The court will overturn the decision only if it determines that there has been a violation of the state constitution, the law was not properly applied, the decision did not comply with the statutes and ordinances, was affected by error of law, or was "[u]nsupported by substantial competent evidence in view of the entire record" or "[a]rbitrary or capricious."[14] The court may affirm the decision, send it back so proper procedure can be followed or additional findings can be made, or order a certain action to be taken, such as issuance or denial of a permit.[15]

1.3.6 Other Land Use Ordinances

New development and changes to existing land uses may be subject to a number of other land use regulations aimed at particular kinds of buildings or land uses. For example, North Carolina's watershed protection legislation is designed to protect water supplies with requirements that apply to the use and development of land. Among other things, this legislation requires local governments to have water supply watershed protection programs that have density requirements,[16] which would include consideration of "impervious surfaces," such as parking lots. State law requires affected local governments to incorporate appropriate land development standards into local zoning, land subdivision, and special-purpose watershed protection ordinances.

Zoning also may include historic districts and a historic preservation commission, and require that a certificate of appropriateness be obtained from the commission before a building within the protected area may be altered or demolished. Another approach is to designate particular landmarks for protection.

Signs and billboards also are regulated with local government zoning. They may be subject to size, illumination, and placement restrictions. Signs along federal highways also may be subject to regulation by the N.C. Department of Transportation.

1.3.7 Exactions

Local governments have increasingly looked to require developers to dedicate land or pay money to local governments to absorb the financial burden of building roads, schools, and public services as a result of new

---

14. G.S. 153A-349(a); G.S. 160A-393(k).
15. G.S. 153A-349(a); G.S. 160A-393(l).
16. G.S. 143-214.5.

construction. These expectations traditionally have been associated with subdivision approval but these days are more often applied to other kinds of zoning actions. The courts have sustained local governments' power to require developers to make off-site improvements or to contribute payments known as *exactions*.

To be legal, exactions must be connected to a legitimate state regulatory interest and not merely a demand for compensation in exchange for a permit. The exaction must be roughly proportional to the development's projected impact. For example, a developer could be required to contribute to the cost of expanding a road intersection made necessary by a commercial project based on an analysis of the additional traffic to be generated by the project.

North Carolina statutes specifically authorize local governments to require developers to make several kinds of improvements, or to contribute funds toward them, as a condition for a land use change approval.[17] The requirement to pay money equal to the estimate of cost for public improvements is called an *impact fee*. The permissible exactions include requiring the developer to contribute land to the public for recreational use, construct streets or pay for their construction, build community service facilities according to local government plans, or reserve land for future school construction.

Often the developer and the local government agree on what the developer will contribute to road or other improvements based on studies about the impact of the proposed development and the need for expansion of public facilities. Local governments usually value successful new developments within their jurisdictions and do not want to discourage them with unreasonable demands. Both local governments and developers understand that agreeing to reasonable accommodations is better than the delay and possible litigation costs of hardened positions and dispute and so usually opt for a cooperative relationship.

1.3.8 Vested Rights

Zoning is aimed at imposing a logical master plan on development. Restrictions apply to future construction. When restrictions are first enacted, owners are not required to remove or modify an existing structure that could not be built according to the new restrictions. An owner is said to have a

---

17. G.S. 153A-331; G.S. 160A-372. .

vested right in continued use of the real estate as it existed when a land use regulation is adopted and to complete a project in progress when regulations change. Local governments may not enact zoning ordinances that compel landowners to stop an existing legal use without raising issues of an unconstitutional deprivation of property without compensation.

There are several legal grounds on which an owner may have a vested right to continued use of an existing structure. One is based on the common law rule that courts have followed that protects an owner who has made substantial lawful investments to carry out a project in good faith reliance on a valid project approval.[18] Such investments that trigger a right can include binding contracts or purchases in reliance on approval, which ordinarily would be based on a building permit issued before the zoning change. Just having a plan for development is not enough. A North Carolina statute also prohibits local governments from denying permits based on a zoning amendment if a valid building permit for the real estate was already issued before the amendment was adopted. This statute applies only to an amendment, not to the initial adoption of a zoning ordinance.[19] Also, an approved site-specific development plan establishes a vested right against the effect of amendments for between two and five years, as determined by the city or county.[20] The local ordinance itself may provide additional grounds for not applying a new or amended land use regulation based on approvals already given or other action undertaken by the owner.

The potential for regulatory changes is of particular concern for large projects that are expected to take several years to complete. To enable both the developer and the regulator to overcome the development disincentives caused by this concern, state law allows local governments and developers to enter into a *development agreement* that essentially guarantees the developer the right to complete a project under the rules in effect at the time of the agreement.[21] The development must be at least twenty-five acres and the agreement must be approved by the local governing body.[22] The agreement must be recorded with the register of deeds.[23]

---

18. Browning-Ferris Indus. of S. Atlantic, Inc. v. Guilford Cnty. Bd. of Adjustment, 126 N.C. App. 168, 171–72, 484 S.E.2d 411, 414 (1997).

19. G.S. 153A-344(b); G.S. 160A-385(b).

20. G.S. 153A-344.1; G.S. 160A-385.1.

21. G.S. 153A-349.1 through .13; G.S. 160A-400.20 through .32.

22. G.S. 153A-349.4; G.S. 153A-349.22; G.S. 160A-400.23 through .32.

23. G.S. 153A-349.11; G.S. 160A-400.30.

1.4 Public Roads

Private real estate ownership is interconnected with the public road system. Road access is essential for use of land, and most land parcels are along a public road or the landowners have a right to get to a road with a deeded easement across someone else's land. The North Carolina public road system to which land use is connected is a complex arrangement of federal, state, and local facilities and responsibilities.

The Federal Highway Administration maintains the interstate highways and other federal highways. The N.C. Department of Transportation maintains state highways and streets outside of municipalities. Inside municipalities, the state maintains major highways and some other roads, and municipalities maintain the other non-federal public roads within their boundaries. The state and municipalities work together to determine whether a particular public road is to be state or municipally maintained.

Federal highways are marked according to a national numbering system. Interstate routes are designed with an "I" on a red-white-and-blue sign; other federal highways with a "U.S." on a white shield. North–south interstate highways have odd numbers, and east–west interstate highways have even numbers. Usually a highway has only two digits (such as I-40 or I-95); three digits are used for bypasses, when a highway loops around a city, with the last two digits the same (such as I-280, I-480, and I-680). North Carolina state highways include primary highways numbered under one thousand. State highways numbered higher than one thousand are secondary. Most secondary roads and municipal roads have names. Municipalities name their own roads. Counties do not maintain roads in North Carolina.

The state and municipalities can acquire rights to land for a road by the same method as a private landowner: by buying it. They also can take the real estate through use of eminent domain in exchange for compensation to the owner for the value of what is taken. Additionally, the state and municipalities can acquire land by *dedication*. Dedication occurs when a real estate owner offers the land for public use and the public authority accepts it. An offer of dedication can be made in a signed document, as commonly occurs when a developer subdivides real estate and the municipality agrees to make the roads public and maintain them. Once a road is accepted, the municipality will hold an easement on the land for the road, and the public will have the right to use it.

There are a variety of other ways that land can become part of the road system. For example, a dedication of land to public use as a road can occur when a developer conveys lots that were subdivided according to a recorded plat that lays out public roads. In such a case, by law the developer is presumed to have offered to dedicate the roads shown on the plat and the municipality has the right to accept them for public use. Public rights to roads also can be acquired by at least twenty years of use by what is known as *prescription* (described in Section 2.3.1.3).

A public road that is in use will have an obvious travel path, usually paved. However, the land subject to public rights usually is wider than the paved portion. Roadway widths vary, but as a typical example two lanes of a road may be twenty-four feet wide, but the right-of-way may be thirty or forty feet wide. A four-lane road may be forty-eight feet wide and the right-of-way sixty feet wide. The additional space may be used as a shoulder or for a sidewalk, signs, or drainage. Or it may merely be kept clear from construction.

Despite the government's right to use the entire width of a right-of-way for travel purposes if it chooses to do so, the owners along the road may have trees, shrubs, and other landscaping as well as mailboxes outside the paved area but within the right-of-way. The owner's right to make improvements to this area, such as to install driveways or culverts, is subject to the government's regulatory powers, and permits usually must be obtained based on satisfaction of conditions. Local regulations also may require that landowners keep the area within the right-of-way in a safe condition, which can include the obligation to trim trees and remove obstructions to vision and public travel. The government itself retains the right to trim or remove trees when necessary for construction or maintenance of the road, as does a utility as part of its easement agreement with the government.

Within municipalities, sidewalks commonly are built within the right-of-way. Governments have the discretion to lay out the sidewalks and maintain control over them, and they have a duty to keep them free from unnecessary obstructions and in proper repair.[24] Although a municipality has a responsibility under state law for the condition of sidewalks within its rights-of-way, someone other than the municipality may be held liable for injuries caused by a defect in the sidewalk if that person created the defect. For example, if a landowner disturbs a sidewalk and creates a safety hazard, that owner may be legally liable for negligence to someone who is injured by the hazard.

---

24. G.S. 160A-296(a).

When the land over which a road runs is held by the government as an easement, the "owners" of the real estate under the road are likely to be the owners who own the land along the road. Real estate that lies along a road and shares a boundary with it is called *abutting* real estate, and its owners are *abutters*. An abutter has a right of access to the public road, but the state or city has the power to regulate points of access as long as the abutter's lot is left with the reasonable possibility of being put to its legal use. In most cases the right of access can be limited to a single point, often called a *curb cut*. More access points to the road may be allowed based on the nature of the real estate and street. Under some circumstances a city may reasonably prohibit any vehicular access points to the road, such as in the midst of a metropolitan area where pedestrian travel can safely be accommodated only if driveways across sidewalks are severely restricted.

If a municipality decides it no longer needs a road it must follow a statutory procedure for its abandonment. The procedure requires notice to the owners of land along the road and a public hearing.[25] Title to the abandoned street or alley is presumed to vest in the owners of adjacent lots to the centerline of the street or alley. This is not a common occurrence, but it does happen, usually as a result of new development that renders continuation of a public road unnecessary.

1.5 Real Estate Taxes

In the United States, state and local governments have always looked to landownership as a source of revenue to pay for public improvements and functions. North Carolina law imposes burdens on property ownership intended to reflect the cost of services that the government provides. In this state two main kinds of taxes are imposed on real estate: the annual real estate tax paid to local governments and the excise tax on conveyances shared by county and state government.

1.5.1 Annual Real Estate Tax

In North Carolina, as in most states, real estate taxes constitute the largest source of revenue for local governments and school districts. In this state, the average tax rate for real estate assessed by the combination of

---

25. G.S. 160A-299.

county and municipal impositions is effectively about 1.1 percent of the real estate's market value, with significantly lower rates in the few areas with a countywide excise tax on conveyances and with combined rates of up to 1.79 percent in a few areas.[26] Local governments can rely on being able to collect real estate taxes because they have legal power to sell owners' real estate to collect taxes if the bills are not paid.

The tax is applied for a fiscal year beginning July 1, and bills are sent soon after that date, but no penalty is imposed as long as the bill is paid by January 5. The bill is sent to whomever was listed as owner as of the preceding January 1. When real estate is sold the buyer and seller customarily *prorate* the taxes by dividing the annual tax by the number of days the buyer and seller each have ownership. So if real estate changes hands early in the calendar year, the seller will be occupying during a period for which taxes have not yet been paid and a credit will be due to the buyer who will later pay the bill. If real estate changes hands later in the year, after the bill has been paid, a prorated amount will be credited to the seller. This is an allocation between the seller and buyer and not payment to the assessing government. The parties' agreement does not affect the local government's ability to pursue those who are responsible for the taxes under the statutes.

The N.C. Constitution exempts from taxation property belonging to the state, counties, and municipal corporations, and it authorizes the General Assembly to exempt from taxation cemeteries and property held for educational, scientific, literary, cultural, charitable, or religious purposes. There are additional exemptions for a limited amount of value in an owner's primary residence. A *homestead exclusion* gives a partial real estate tax reduction for elderly or disabled low-income people who own their own homes. Land actually used for agricultural, horticultural, or forestry purposes that meets certain ownership and size requirements is eligible for taxation based on its value in present use, even though it may have a greater market value for other uses, such as commercial development.

The real estate tax is based on market value, as determined by a periodic appraisal that takes into account the real estate's characteristics. The tax is called *ad valorem*, which means according to value. The goal is not to get the market value exactly right, which can never be so because market values are constantly changing, but to make the tax on any given real estate

---

26. North Carolina Department of Revenue, County Property Tax Rates and Revaluation Schedules (Fiscal Year 2011–2012), *available at* www.dor.state.nc.us/publications/countyrates.html.

proportional to every other comparable taxable real estate. It is this pro-portionality—rather than the amount—that is required constitutionally in North Carolina as is required generally in the country.

All counties must reassess real estate at least every eight years to adjust for changes in real estate values and the market. A taxpayer may challenge the valuation by appealing to the county board of equalization or, in some counties, to the board of commissioners. The board convenes each year in April and at its first meeting may vote to close the window for accepting appeal applications and deal only with those that have been submitted by that date. The N.C. Property Tax Commission hears appeals from these boards across the state. On an appeal the county's appraisal is presumed to be correct, but an owner can get an adjustment by proving that the value is excessive or disproportionate to comparable properties. The owner may appeal the commission's decision to the N.C. Court of Appeals and the N.C. Supreme Court, but those courts usually choose not to hear tax appeals.

Failure to pay tax that is overdue can result in a forced sale of the real estate to collect. Tax collectors also have broad authority to enforce the payment of delinquent taxes by seizing personal property and attaching bank accounts.

1.5.2 Excise Tax

Another significant tax collected in connection with real estate is the *excise tax* on conveyances. This is sometimes called a *transfer tax*. Before a deed for which a tax is due may be recorded, the excise tax must be paid and the deed marked by the register of deeds to show this has occurred.[27] By statute the seller owes the tax, but it is paid to the register of deeds by the person presenting the deed for recording. The tax reporting procedure creates an odd dynamic because although the seller is responsible for paying the tax, the buyer or the buyer's legal representative usually presents the deed and pays the tax. The county may bring an enforcement action for failure to pay a tax that was owed, and an intentional misrepresentation about what was paid for the real estate could be tax fraud and subject the offender to civil and criminal penalties.

The excise tax is levied on conveyances of an interest in real estate by all persons and organizations except federal, state, county, and municipal

---

27. G.S. 105-228.28 through .37.

governments and their *instrumentalities*, bodies formed by governments for public purposes. Roughly half is retained by the county with the remainder paid to the state. The current rate is two-tenths of one percent of what was paid for the real estate. If someone pays by exchanging property rather than by paying cash, the tax will be based on the value of what is exchanged. If the owners of two separate parcels trade property, the value of the property being exchanged is considered payment and the excise tax is required. There is no deduction for an assumed loan or other obligation secured by the property. If the amount paid for the real estate is not a multiple of $500, the amount of value is rounded up to the next multiple of $500 before computing the tax. If the land lies in more than one county, the excise tax must be paid to the county where the most valuable part of the land lies. Timber deeds and contracts also are subject to the excise tax. There is no excise tax if the real estate is a gift or no payment is made for it.[28]

The state excise tax does not apply when the transfer is made upon someone's death by will or the laws of intestacy that provide rules about who inherits when there is no will. It also does not apply to a transfer by what the statute calls "operation of law," which occurs when no instrument of conveyance is necessary—for example, when a joint tenant succeeds after the other joint tenant dies or when real estate passes to another as a consequence of the life tenant's death. The tax also does not apply to a lease or a deed of trust.[29] When a husband and wife separate and as part of a divorce property settlement one spouse conveys to the other, the spouse who receives the deed is treated as receiving real estate he or she already owns, and no excise tax is due on the transaction.

Probably the most common question that arises about application of the tax concerns transfers from an investor in an entity to the entity itself, such as when someone forms a corporation and transfers real estate to the corporation in exchange for shares. This is a transfer for consideration—the value of the shares—and the tax therefore applies. There is no statutory exception for this kind of transfer.

The tax does not apply to an entity that is merging, converting, or consolidating according to a statutory procedure. When a deed conveys real estate as part of a plan of reorganization under Chapter 11 of the federal

---

28. G.S. 105-228.29; G.S. 105-228.30(a).
29. G.S. 105-228.29.

Bankruptcy Code, by federal law no excise tax may be charged.[30] This exclusion does not apply to other transfers by bankrupt debtors, such as those that might occur before the reorganization or that occur in liquidation.

Several counties have an additional excise tax, sometimes referred to as a *land transfer tax*, of not more than $1 per $100 of consideration or value on instruments conveying interests in land. This tax applies in the same way as the statewide excise tax and must be paid before the register of deeds may record an instrument of conveyance. A statute makes any *county* excise tax inapplicable to transfers made as a result of foreclosure or by a deed in lieu of foreclosure, an exception also set forth in the acts authorizing the tax. This does not eliminate the need to pay the *statewide* excise tax collectible in all counties as a result of foreclosure or by a deed in lieu of foreclosure, and that tax is due on the amount paid or credited for the real estate.[31]

1.6 Eminent Domain

Notwithstanding the firmly established notion of private property rights, American law has always sustained the power of federal, state, and local governments to use *eminent domain* to take real estate for use as roads, public buildings, and other public improvements provided that just compensation is paid to the owner for what is taken. Use of the eminent domain power to take real estate also is called *condemnation*, regardless of the real estate's condition. As the demand for public improvements has intensified and government projects have become more interrelated with private development, some particular uses of eminent domain have been questioned and challenged, but the use of the power for public projects has been a recognized legislative power for centuries. Most of the disputes that arise over eminent domain are disagreements about the amount of compensation that must be paid to the owner, not about the constitutionality of the power itself.

---

30. 11 U.S.C. § 1146(c) (2006).
31. G.S. 45-45.2.

1.6.1 Who Has Eminent Domain Power

No government agency or public utility has a power of eminent domain unless the federal or a state legislature authorizes it. Whenever a utility or local government exercises eminent domain, it does so through the delegated authority of the elected state representatives. The N.C. General Assembly has delegated this power to public entities and private enterprises providing public services at the state and local levels.

At the state level, the Department of Transportation has the power of eminent domain to acquire land for highways and for constructing and maintaining the highway system.[32] The Department of Administration has eminent domain power for many state government functions, such as overseeing state buildings and other governmental facilities, parks and forestry, historical sites, public waterway access and preservation, and hazardous waste facilities.[33] State statutes authorize local governments to use eminent domain to acquire real estate for use in carrying out their most common functions involving schools, roads and sidewalks, parking, parks, hospitals, libraries, cemeteries, office buildings, water and sewer systems, and a few other specified purposes. Municipalities and counties also have the power of eminent domain to acquire land for other public purposes, such as public transportation systems, water supply, storm and waste water management, airports, historic property, cable television, electricity, gas, housing, and redevelopment. Coastal counties and municipalities have been authorized to use eminent domain for certain beach access and maintenance purposes. The statutes also authorize a number of state and local public agencies, public utilities, and other authorities to use eminent domain to acquire real estate for their authorized purposes.[34]

Under certain circumstances government authorities may use eminent domain to take real estate because it is in such bad condition that it constitutes a "blighted" parcel under the law. This requires that the targeted property have specified characteristics, such as conditions that endanger life or property.[35]

The courts generally have deferred to the legislatures about when the use of eminent domain is sufficiently tied to a public use or benefit. In *Kelo v.*

---

32. G.S. 136-19.
33. G.S. 146-22.1; G.S. 146-24.1.
34. G.S. 40A-3.
35. G.S. 160A-515; G.S. 160A-503(2a).

City of New London,[36] a 2005 case that elicited much public comment, the U.S. Supreme Court held that the Fifth Amendment was not violated when the eminent domain power was used to acquire land through a government's appointed development agent for conveyance to a private party. The land was to be part of an integrated plan developed by the government to rejuvenate an economically troubled area. This decision reflected the Court's deferential approach to reviewing legislative acts authorizing eminent domain. The N.C. Supreme Court also has been deferential to the state legislature's delegation of eminent domain power. The court has held that eminent domain may be used to acquire property that the public will not functionally "use" without offending the state constitution if the purpose satisfies a "public benefit test" by contributing to the general welfare and prosperity of the public at large.

The courts have also held that authorities with the power of eminent domain have discretion to determine the property to be taken if the purpose is legislatively authorized and constitutionally permissible. Decisions about project needs are not subject to court approval except when facts indicate that the government is acting in bad faith on no conceivably legitimate basis. North Carolina's courts presume that public officials act legally and in good faith. For example, the courts will not scrutinize a decision to widen a street without a showing of bad faith or obvious abuse of discretion. An owner has the burden of proving that an abuse of discretion has occurred. These presumptions are based on an acknowledgment that public officials must be given some discretion to carry out their duties if reasonable people can be expected to assume such responsibilities, and public administration would be made very difficult if the courts intensely supervised choices about how to go about delivering public improvements.

1.6.2 Compensation

When property is taken by the government both the federal and state constitutions require that "just compensation" be paid to the owner. *Just compensation* means payment of the market value of what is taken. This is based on the acquired property's potential "highest and best use," not just its current use or uses that its current owners are considering. It is what a hypothetical willing buyer and a hypothetical informed buyer considering such possibilities would pay. The usual approach to figuring this out for

---

36. 545 U.S. 469 (2005).

residential properties is market comparison, by which appraisers identify neighborhoods with properties similar to the subject parcel, research recent sales information, and make adjustments for differences in lot and building size and characteristics.

When only a part of a tract of land is acquired for a public project, such as a strip along a roadway, the value of the remainder of the tract could be diminished. This could result from the remaining area being less than what it was or from what is being constructed. For example, towers and high-voltage wires could have a negative impact on a home. For takings by a local government, compensation is the greater of two measures. The first is the amount by which the value of the entire tract before the taking exceeds the value of the remainder after the taking. The second is the value of what is taken. In takings by the state Department of Transportation and other authorities authorized to use the state procedure, the measure of damages for a partial taking is the difference in value for the remainder without the option of the value of the property taken.

An authority with eminent domain power has the option of taking a right to use the property rather than its full ownership. As described in Section 2.3, an easement interest is a right to limited use of or a restriction on another's land. A typical kind of easement is a right to cross another's land for a driveway or a utility's right to cross property with power lines that serve the real estate or other utility users. Eminent domain authorities also may acquire temporary easement rights to store equipment and materials or to cross property during construction of public improvements. With such an easement the authority will pay rent for the use of the real estate during the construction, and ownership and control fully returns to the owner when the project is completed.

A common issue involving an owner's claim to compensation involves tree trimming by government authorities. A government may trim and cut trees along a roadway in fulfilling its responsibility to maintain streets, provided the work is done reasonably and in good faith. They may remove trees that impede travel because such conditions may be considered a nuisance to the public's right of travel. But a landowner may have a claim to compensation if tree destruction or damage was not reasonably intended to protect the public. Such claims are unusual.

Local government eminent domain cases commonly involve road construction and expansion that affect the public road access of privately owned parcels. An owner is not entitled to compensation merely because some of the passing traffic has been diminished by a change in configuration because nearly every owner would be entitled to compensation whenever improvements were made to reduce hazards. Access restrictions, median installation, and other changes that control travel can be undertaken pursuant to the police power without triggering any obligation to pay compensation for the common effect of such measures. If direct access to a highway has been eliminated or substantially interfered with, the landowner may be entitled to damages. Only a change that substantially impairs convenient access to the real estate is compensable unless a statute authorizes payment for less serious changes. Compensation is based on the effect of the change. There may be no right to compensation if other available routes are sufficient to support the real estate's most valuable use.

When government takes the land on which a business is operated and the owners must move or curtail their operations, the owners may believe that they are losing future business profits. North Carolina law does not require compensation to be paid for lost profits in such a circumstance.

1.6.3 Eminent Domain Procedure

In the typical situation involving the potential for use of eminent domain power, the condemning authority will contact the owner and first attempt to reach an agreement for purchase of what is needed. Typically the authority will obtain at least a brief report from an appraiser to show the owner how the amount being offered is fair. If an agreement cannot be reached, a court action will be filed to have the amount of compensation determined.

Local government authorities are required to send each owner written notice of the action at least thirty days before an action is begun in court.[37] Authorities with eminent domain power may go on the real estate before filing any action to conduct tests.[38] The thirty-day notice does not apply to the state Department of Transportation procedure.

At the time the eminent domain case is filed, the condemning authority must deposit the estimated amount of just compensation. The owner may withdraw this amount without losing the ability to prove that more must be paid. Most eminent domain cases are only about the amount of compensation because rarely is there any basis to challenge the authority for the taking. During the eminent domain case, the parties will exchange information about their claims and positions, including how they value

---

37. G.S. 40A-40.
38. G.S. 40A-11; G.S. 136-120.

the property being acquired. The court will decide legal issues about what property is being taken, the proper parties, or competing claims to the deposit. The issue of just compensation will be submitted to a jury if a jury was demanded by either party, or the parties can elect to have the issue decided by three appointed commissioners or by a judge. After all the issues have been decided, final judgment will be entered, which will be filed with the register of deeds to reflect the transfer of ownership. The authority will pay to the owner any amounts still owed for just compensation to the extent not already paid by withdrawal from the deposit. The parties may be able to reach an agreement on the amount of compensation at any time during an eminent domain proceeding.

The law enables governments that need to use eminent domain to acquire real estate to move forward with projects without having to wait for a final resolution of disputes about how much compensation must be paid to the owner. Under North Carolina law, most acquisitions are by this *quick take* procedure, by which the government becomes the owner and entitled to possession of the real estate as soon it files a declaration and makes the deposit of compensation with the court. The quick-take procedure applies to acquisitions for roads, sidewalks, schools, and utilities, among other purposes. If the government is taking real estate for purposes to which the quick-take procedure does not apply, in most cases the government will become the owner of the real estate when the owner files an answer.

1.6.4 Deprivation of Property without Procedure

Sometimes owners believe they have been deprived of their property by government activity without an eminent domain procedure. This is called *inverse condemnation* because the owner rather than the government must initiate the court procedure for compensation. In modern times governments and utilities rarely take someone's property outright without following the eminent domain procedure. More likely a claim arises from a claim of excessive regulation, when government imposes a restriction so severe that the owner believes the property has been taken for public benefit. For example, a successful inverse condemnation claim was made when a coastal protection law effectively prevented a waterfront lot owner from any construction or economically viable use of the property,[39] and

---

39. Lucas v. S. Carolina Coastal Council, 505 U.S. 1003 (1992).

when local regulators insisted that as a condition for expansion of a store a landowner had to contribute land for a public bicycle path without any demonstration that the need for the path was being generated by the proposed construction.[40]

The law tries to distinguish between the effect of government activities that have an impact on properties generally and those that unusually affect particular properties and constitutionally entitle owners to compensation. For example, the courts have held that the owners of land along a highway are not entitled to compensation just because changes are made to restrict travel, but an owner may be so entitled if negatively affected in a particular and substantial way. This might occur, for example, if road changes entirely cut off a lot from access to the public way.

To make an inverse condemnation claim the owner must file an action against the government. The damages that would be paid are calculated by the same method as eminent domain. There is a strict time limit for making a claim for compensation. For most such claims a specific procedure must be followed, and the action must be filed within two years after the occupation or use first occurred.[41]

---

40. Dolan v. City of Tigard, 512 U.S. 374 (1994).
41. G.S. 40A-51.

2 Shared Interests and Boundaries

When people think of owning real estate they most commonly think of a house on a private lot. Many think of a private space in an apartment, townhouse, or condominium unit. These spaces invoke thoughts of boundaries in the sense of lines or walls that separate, but they also involve the rights of others on the opposite side of those lines and walls that may affect how the lot or unit can be used. There are many other aspects of the notion of boundaries; real estate ownership can be separated and shared in other, less geographic ways. One of the reasons real estate law can be so mysterious is that ownership arrangements are infinitely variable. Subject to the kind of government regulations that are summarized in Chapter 1, owners are free to share or divide their rights and obligations in any way they choose. This chapter introduces the basics of the most frequently encountered ways in which ownership is separated and shared. These include how more than one person can be the owner, how boundaries are defined, and how shared use can result in a change of ownership. This chapter also provides a summary of the common ways in which ownership of adjoining lots or units can be arranged to share benefits and burdens, including easements, restrictive covenants, leases, planned communities, condominiums, time shares, and life estates. Finally, this chapter provides an overview of the laws of nuisance and trespass and how they address unauthorized shared use.

2.1 Owners and Co-Owners

Most people and companies who become real estate owners do so by paying a prior owner and receiving and recording a deed. The recorded deed enables others to identify the owner or owners. If there is more than one owner, the deed usually will use time-tested forms of co-ownership. Although these forms and the rights they entail are well-known to real estate lawyers, they may not be understood even by those who have these rights.

2.1.1 Co-Ownership

Most co-ownership arrangements are in traditional forms that are governed by well-established rules for what each owner has and what happens when any one owner dies. When a deed uses the appropriate terminology for one of these forms, such as *tenancy by the entireties* or *joint tenancy with right of survivorship*, it will carry with it all of the legal rules that apply to such a form without their having to be expressed in the deed. Nothing in the law limits anyone to these established forms of ownership—what will be acceptable is up to those who transfer and receive the real estate. But a clear benefit of using customary forms of ownership is that everyone can understand what the rules are. Being creative is appropriate when something unusual is being described, but in such a case the drafter must be clear. When something customary is being described creatively, those who later attempt to interpret the language may not understand what was intended, and ambiguity may be resolved with legal presumptions that the drafter did not consider.

Deeds form a chain of ownership; the interests of all in the chain depend on what their predecessors received. Sometimes a deed must be interpreted long after those who were involved are gone. Even when common forms of ownership are used, confusion can arise. This occurs, for example, if there are discrepancies in the way a name appears on the deed by which the real estate was received and the deed by which it is later transferred. Obvious typographical errors usually do not create a problem if the variation can be easily explained, such as when someone adopts a new name after marriage or divorce. On rare occasions an error results in a dispute and there is need for a court interpretation of what was intended.

Tenancy by the entireties is the most common form of co-ownership in North Carolina. Real estate owned by a husband and wife together is usually held in this form because its use ensures that each spouse has rights to the real estate and that one spouse cannot convey without the other's participation. If one spouse dies during ownership, the other automatically becomes sole owner. This is the most important practical consideration of this form of ownership, known as the *right of survivorship*. Also, neither spouse may convey or mortgage the real estate without the other's participation.

Two or more owners who are not spouses can own property in another form that has a right of survivorship, known as *joint tenancy*. Each joint tenant has full ownership rights, and when one dies the other automatically becomes sole owner. Another form of co-ownership, *tenancy in common*, is used when co-owners do not want a right of survivorship. With this form, one owner's share can be conveyed to another separately, and it separately passes to the owner's heirs upon the owner's death. Unless otherwise specified, tenants in common are presumed to have equal interests, such as one-half interests when there are two tenants in common. By statute, unless a deed specifies a joint tenancy, a conveyance to two or more persons will create a tenancy in common.[1] The intent to create joint tenancy will be demonstrated "if the instrument creating the joint tenancy expressly provides for a right of survivorship."[2] When a deed is to two or more individuals without specifying the form in which they are taking ownership, they are presumed to be tenants in common unless something different is made clear.

2.1.2 Entities as Owners

Just as individual human beings may acquire, hold, and transfer real estate in their own names, so can legal entities, the most common being corporations, limited liability companies, and voluntary corporations. Entities continue to have the power to transfer property in liquidation of their businesses even after they have been legally dissolved by agreement of the shareholders or members, by order of a court, or administratively by failing to comply with statutory requirements, such as filing reports and paying fees. This authority becomes important when the company fails to fully wind up its business. When these entities have been dissolved without a transfer of real estate, difficult legal issues can arise about exactly what types of documents are needed to transfer it because, among other things, it may be unclear which individuals have continuing rights in the dissolved entity.

---

1. Section 41-2 of the North Carolina General Statutes (hereinafter G.S.).
2. *Id.*

Knowing the basics of the most common entities is helpful for identifying them when their names appear on legal instruments and for understanding how they own and transfer real estate.

A corporation is a traditional form of business entity favored because it allows the accumulation of capital through the sale of stock and bonds and it limits shareholder liability to the extent of their investments in the corporation. A corporation exists only after the necessary steps have been taken for incorporation with a state governing authority. For a North Carolina corporation these steps include the filing of articles of incorporation with the N.C. Department of the Secretary of State. The entity's name must include the word "corporation," "incorporated," "company," or "limited" or the abbreviation "corp.", "inc.", "co.", or "ltd." North Carolina corporations must have an identified registered agent in this state to whom someone may send legal notices. A professional corporation is a corporation in which the stock must be owned and held only by licensees of particular professional services, such as lawyers, accountants, surveyors, architects, physicians, dentists, or veterinarians. The shareholders, directors, and officers of a professional corporation are not individually liable for errors or omissions of the other shareholders, directors, or officers in the corporation. Its name must include the words *professional association* (P.A.) or *professional corporation* (P.C.). A nonprofit corporation also is created with the filing of articles of incorporation, and it may enter into contracts, own property, and incur liabilities to the same extent as an individual and generally has the same attributes and requirements as a business corporation.

The limited liability company is a popular business form because it offers the liability protections of corporations, the tax advantages of partnerships, and the ease and flexibility of formation. North Carolina limited liability companies are formed with articles of organization filed with the Department of the Secretary of State. Its name must include the words "limited liability company," "ltd. liability co.," "limited liability co.," or "ltd. liability company" or the abbreviation "L.L.C." or "LLC." The company is comprised of members, who automatically are considered to be managers unless the articles of organization provide otherwise.

Partnerships also can be property owners, in the name of the partnership or in the partners' names. If the deed is to the partnership in the partnership name, then the property can be transferred only in the same way. Partners have interests similar to those of a joint tenancy. Unless otherwise specified, each partner has equal rights to partnership property for partnership purposes. An apparently authorized act of a partner in the name of the partnership will bind the partnership unless the person with whom the partner is acting actually knows the partner had no authority. This means that partners should be clear with each other and those whom they deal if individual partners' authority is intended to be restricted. Limited partnerships also may own property, as tenants in partnership. General partners in limited partnerships have the same powers as partners in general partnerships.

Unlike a general or ordinary partnership, a North Carolina limited partnership cannot exist without a certificate of limited partnership executed and filed with the Department of the Secretary of State. Its name must contain the words "limited partnership" or "ltd. partnership" or the abbreviation "L.P." or "LP." North Carolina limited partnerships are required to have a registered office and agent in North Carolina. The general partner of a limited partnership has the power and authority to bind the entity. There are specialized forms of partnerships, such as registered limited liability partnerships, which are used only rarely in specialized projects.

Another common form of ownership is a trust. A trust is not a legal entity but, rather, an agreement between someone transferring property or rights to another with the intent that it be held for the transferor's benefit. The person who transfers the property right is called the *settlor* or *grantor*. The person with whom the property is entrusted is called the *trustee*. Trustees are usually individuals, but they may be institutions, such as banks. Most trust agreements also identify successor trustees who step in if the original trustee resigns or dies. The person or entity for whose benefit the property is entrusted is called the *beneficiary*. Trusts are governed by *trust agreements*, which may be separate documents or contained within wills. Trustees, as fiduciaries, are subject to strict statutory and common law obligations. When property is to be held in a trust, it is transferred to the trustee, and the deed identifies the trust agreement and mentions the fact that the person is a trustee. The trustee will also transfer the property according to the trust agreement provisions. If the trustee has changed, the deed or another instrument will describe this change.

Religious organizations may appoint trustees to acquire, hold, and convey property in trust for a church, denomination, religious society, or congregation. They may act also through their ecclesiastical officers.

These are common types of organizations or entities. There are other organizations authorized by state or federal law, each of which has its own applicable laws and rules.

2.2 Boundaries, Descriptions, and Plats

A *boundary* is a shared line on the ground, a place where different owner-ship interests meet. While owners on either side of that line may have rights that derive from entirely different sources, these rights are inextricably linked together. Usually a boundary is both a physically visible line and a legal line, but sometimes the two are at different places. A simple example of this is a fence that is put not along the line based on the descriptions in the neighbors' deeds, but at a location someone incorrectly thought was the legal boundary. Knowing where the legal line is requires understanding deeds and plans and their legal effect. Sometimes this involves compli-cated legal questions, such as how to resolve a discrepancy when the neigh-bors have legal boundaries in their deeds that do not coincide. Although such discrepancies are unusual, they do arise, and their resolution usually requires legal expertise and sometimes court action.

2.2.1 Boundary Descriptions

The starting point for determining where a legal boundary exists is the deeds by which the adjoining owners acquired their interests. Deed bound-ary descriptions vary in technique, ranging from precise measurements depicted on a survey, as is used in modern conveyances of newly subdivided real estate, to vague mention of neighboring real estate owners, as is typical of descriptions used centuries ago and sometimes carried forward to today. Regardless of how the boundaries are described in a deed, the proper goal of the drafter is to create a clear record of the intended boundary locations as well as to match the description to the legal rights based on prior convey-ances in the chains of title.

Some deeds describe what is being conveyed merely by referring to the deed by which the person selling the real estate acquired it. This approach ensures that nothing is left out or incorrectly assumed to be added. But such incorporation by reference requires the person receiving the deed to examine other documents to see a description of the boundaries. Another common method is to refer to a plat for a description, which also requires looking at another document to see the boundaries. A risk with this approach is that an unexpected boundary or possible problem may be overlooked if the plat is not carefully examined. If the plat is not recorded, the deed description can become problematic if the public record does not otherwise contain sufficient information to tell what was intended. Older deeds sometimes refer to unrecorded plats, and problems can arise, but this is rare in modern conveyances.

Another common method for describing a boundary, especially in older deeds, is by *metes and bounds*. This is a description of the real estate's geometric shape by reference to points and distances. A typical metes and bounds description starts at a specified *point of beginning* and proceeds clockwise or counterclockwise around the real estate's boundaries giving distances and courses for each segment. An image of the property can be created by tracing out the lines and angles to scale.

Centuries ago, boundaries were commonly described only by reference to neighbors or very general terrain features. Unfortunately many older deeds mentioned landmarks that could have since moved or disappeared, such as meandering rivers, crosses cut into rocks, or tree stumps. These references can result in confusion and dispute, and there have been many cases in which the resolution of boundary questions depended on extensive research based on artifacts and expert surveyor opinion about marking techniques used over the years. Descriptions based on carefully installed and recorded artificial monuments, such as concrete posts, provide a much more reliable type of boundary evidence. Modern artificial monuments are set at boundary corners and at the beginning and end of curves, with identifying information about the surveyor or engineer who installed them.

2.2.2 Plats

Descriptions provided in deeds are for determining legal boundaries. Although a deed description may give a sense of geometry and distance, it may not be enough to determine where the boundary is on the ground in relation to other properties. For this purpose, a *plat*, also known as a plan, is the proverbial picture worth a thousand words. Plats show not only boundaries of the real estate about which the plat is drawn, but also where this real estate is in relation to physical boundary markers, roads, structures, and other properties.

A plat can be something as simple as a drawing attached to a deed. In modern transactions, especially for recently subdivided parcels, a plat will be prepared by a surveyor according to professional standards. These standards are intended to ensure that the information shown on a plat is as accurate as possible and that surveyors take into account that the information is relevant to more than the subject parcel, including to later owners and neighbors.

Surveyors and engineers are required to put certifications and seals on their plats to show compliance with requirements and regulations, which in this state are issued by the N.C. Board of Examiners for Engineers and Surveyors. To receive a license, they must satisfy educational and experiential requirements and pass an examination.[3] Surveyors do not determine real estate ownership or property rights. They provide investigation, measurement, and evaluation involving land, reference points, and boundaries. Surveyors who have experience with properties of the nature involved— for example, urban or rural—and in the same vicinity as the subject real estate may have especially valuable insights into boundary issues based on what they know. Engineers and architects also draw plans in connection with land and structures, but they do not investigate or locate boundaries. Engineers are licensed to design structures, utilities, and systems, and architects are licensed to design buildings. Many developments involve surveyors, engineers, and architects working collaboratively.

A type of survey often encountered in real estate transactions is what is called an ALTA or ALTA/ACSM title survey. The American Land Title Association (in collaboration with the American Congress on Surveying and Mapping) and the National Society of Professional Surveyors (NSPS) jointly issue criteria for ALTA surveys. These standards specify the information to be shown, including boundaries, buildings, fences, and other features. They require surveyors to make notes of certain possible issues, such as if the survey reveals a boundary that differs significantly from the record or the possibility of an easement that cannot be located. They also require surveyors to note possible encroaching structures across boundaries. These requirements are intended to alert insurers, lenders, and owners to possible problems. A survey prepared to comply with these requirements will contain the caption ALTA/ACSM LAND TITLE SURVEY and a certification that the plat complies with these requirements.

Although plats vary in what they show according to their purpose and the preparer's approach, most have similar features that, if understood, can be helpful to someone trying to learn about the real estate that is depicted. An important first step when reviewing a plat is to look at the *title box*, which usually is at the bottom center or bottom right. This should show for whom the plat was prepared, which indicates its focus. While a plat

---

3. G.S. Chapter 89C.

may provide useful information regarding any boundary shown on it, the information about the property that is the focus of the plat is likely to be more complete and detailed. The title box also may describe the purpose of the survey. For new construction and in many other instances, a new instrument survey is necessary to ensure that the boundaries taken from the title documents are correct and that there are no new problems that have arisen, such as newly constructed structures that cross boundaries. For some purposes, such as a single boundary line adjustment, the owners may be able to have only one line newly measured and marked. A plat that is prepared based on limited research should describe the scope of the undertaking and indicate the extent to which information from unverified sources is being included. A subdivision plat will likely show boundaries, roads, easements, utility routes, and a lot of other information required by local land use regulators as a condition for approval. A boundary line adjustment plat, on the other hand, may show only one particular boundary, and the rest of the information may be taken from another plat.

Any plat is best understood when the parcel configuration is oriented from a familiar perspective, which can be done by looking at both the boundaries and the north arrow on the plat. The plat likely situates the parcel within a small vicinity map to show the parcel in broad relationship to identifiable roads. The scale will show the relationship between distances on the plat and distances on the ground. Naturally the scale will depend on how large an area is being shown; if a large area is shown, just a little distance on the plat will be much more than if a small area is shown.

Plats are also best understood by careful, methodical examination of all the information that appears on them. For example, boundary lines should be considered in relation to structures, roads, natural features, and adjoining parcels. The distances that are shown will be informative not only for a sense of relative size, but also for revealing variations between what is said in a deed and what is measured on the ground. Information about monuments also should be studied. If there is a discrepancy, such as boundary information taken from deeds that overlaps or leaves a gap, or structures that cross over boundaries, these may be apparent by looking at the lines and shapes as well as in notes on the plat. Plats also will show utility lines, easements, roads, and other features and can reveal boundaries that do not seem to match, or buildings or fences that cross over lot lines.

Notes on plats can be overlooked as uninteresting fine print, but they often contain important information. Such notes may appear anywhere on the plat but usually appear as a series of notes along the side of the sheet. They may contain standard information that is not helpful, but they also can reveal another's claim to the real estate or a problem with the boundaries. For example, a note on a plat could mention a possible easement that cannot be drawn because it cannot be precisely located, or a note may raise a question about the accuracy of a deed description. In any event, notes are part of the big picture available for understanding the nature of the subject real estate.

2.3 Easements

People tend to think of real estate ownership as an exclusive right to a structure and the land surrounding it. But private ownership does not necessarily mean isolation from neighbors. Easements are a common method for a developer or cooperative landowners to build a community of interrelated uses. They allow someone to have the benefit of limited use of another's real estate. One common type of easement is a right-of-way to walk or drive over a private road or over one lot to get to another. Easements also can be given to each owner in a community to restrict owners from doing something on their property, such as building a structure that is incompatible with the neighborhood or cutting down trees that preserve a natural aspect of the community. Developers accomplish this by prescribing permissible uses or structures in an enforceable easement agreement recorded in the register of deeds.

The most common type of easement allows utility lines to cross real estate. When sewer, water, and other utilities are run in a neighborhood, the developer will reserve easements across the lots and common areas to allow the utilities to be brought to individual properties. The following is an example of basic language that might be used to create a typical utility line easement, with details to be spelled out more precisely with additional clauses:

> A perpetual easement with the right to install, maintain, remove, and restore a sewer line, and to clear and maintain the easement area free of structures, trees, shrubs, undergrowth, and obstructions, together with the right to enter the easement area for such purposes, within the route as shown on the plat . . .

There are many details to consider in creating such easements, such as the extent to which the use can be expanded, the right to enter the easement area for maintenance, and the right to replace the facility if it fails or needs an upgrade. As another example, an easement to devote real estate to conservation may be created with a document that describes the real estate and its restrictions, beginning with this kind of general language:

> The grantor shall preserve the property in perpetuity in its natural ecosystem and habitat of fish, wildlife, trees, and plants . . .

Such protected area easements are becoming increasingly common, and their details vary with the owner's intent.

Another common type of easement is for lots to use private roads within a subdivision. Unless a municipality takes control of the subdivision roads, the owners may depend on easement rights to get to the public road system. These rights are likely to be described in the deeds to the lots and shown on the subdivision plat. A recorded instrument should describe the nature of the access rights and who has the obligation to maintain the roads. Most likely the developer initially will have maintenance responsibilities, but these will shift to a homeowners association and the costs passed along to the lot owners. Because such arrangements are subject to problems if the developer does not meet its responsibilities and if the owners incur unexpected costs, modern developers usually seek to have the subdivision roads accepted by the municipality to be publicly maintained.

Neighbors commonly use easements for driveways. Such an arrangement may be required for development when land use regulations limit the number of driveway access points to the public road. Shared driveways can become problematic unless the neighbors understand their mutual obligations and responsibilities and adhere to them in good faith. Many disputes arise after owners convey their properties to others who do not share a common understanding about the appropriate nature of the use and the parties' responsibilities.

Easements also are a mechanism for ensuring common enjoyment of a variety of beneficial land uses within a subdivision. For example, subdivisions along an ocean or a lake may include a common beach. Easements may be part of the arrangement for access to the waterfront and for defining obligations and setting rules. By designating areas that may not be excavated or deforested, easements are also used to maintain the topography in such a condition to prevent flooding and erosion.

As noted above, easements can be used to restrict someone's use of land. Landowners, conservation groups, and land use regulators employ easement agreements to address environmental concerns. A *conservation easement* is a commitment to maintain land in its natural state. This commitment is made with an instrument recorded with the register of deeds. Years ago, due to a historic reluctance to allow land to be restricted by someone who is not legally connected to that land, concerns were raised about the enforceability of conservation easements when the rights to enforce it were not held by a neighbor. Today conservation agreements are widely recognized as enforceable even if they do not directly benefit another particular lot or person. In addition to easements that require land to be kept in its natural state, easements also can be used to restrict land to a particular kind of use, such as agricultural or forestry, or to require its preservation as a historic use.[4] Such restrictions are enforceable through court action, but recorded conservation easements are conspicuous features of the real estate to which they apply, and they often enhance the desirability and economic value of other parts of the real estate and the neighborhood.

An easement can be used to accomplish an infinite variety of other purposes involving the use of land. Although easements are helpful for owners to make better use of real estate than might otherwise be possible, they also are among the most common subjects of legal disputes involving real estate. When real estate is subject to an easement, the landowner's natural inclination over time is to want to curtail the burden of its use, and the easement beneficiary's natural inclination is to want to expand the use. Easements often originate when land is first subdivided or between friendly neighbors when the outlook is cooperative and disagreements seem unlikely. Later owners may not be as conciliatory as those who agreed to the easement, and disagreement may arise about the details of rights and obligations. Another common cause of dispute about an easement results when there is a change in use as a result of changes or expansions. A serious challenge when creating easements is not only to address current conditions but also to try to predict changes in the nature of the real estate use and the owners' and users' interests.

---

4. G.S. 121-34 through -42.

2.3.1 Creation of Easements

Easements usually originate with a deliberate development plan in which they are defined by rules in an instrument recorded at the office of the register of deeds. This instrument spells out the details of the rights and obligations of the owner of the real estate being subjected to the easement and of those who are intended to have use of it. One aspect of easements that makes them a frequent subject of disagreement, and sometimes of litigation, is that they also can arise by other methods recognized under the law. These other methods of easement creation include by implication in the way real estate has been subdivided and by a history of actual use that becomes a permanent right.

2.3.1.1 Easements Described in Instruments

Easements are often generated as part of a comprehensive development scheme designed by a developer for such things as subdivision roads, utility and sewer lines, drainage, and common area facilities. This can be done with the deeds that first transfer the subdivided lots or in a separate instrument that will apply to later conveyances and incorporated into the deeds making them. A lot subject to an easement commonly is called a *burdened lot*, whereas the lot with the benefit of an easement commonly is called a *benefited lot*. A variety of titles are used on the different instruments that create easements, such as "Easement Deed, "Easement Agreement," "Declaration of Easement," or "Declaration of Covenants."

Sometimes an easement connects only two parcels, such as when someone divides real estate into two lots and reserves a right to cross one with a driveway or utility line to reach the other. This kind of easement is likely to be described in the first deed being used to convey one of the parcels to a new owner, in which case the deed will state that one lot is "subject to" an easement "reserved" to the other. The easement will then be mentioned in later deeds of conveyance for the benefited and burdened properties. Unless the document defining the easement states that its duration is limited to a certain number of years or until a certain event, its burdens and benefits will pass with transfers of the affected properties, whether by deed or as a result of death. Owners creating easements have the power to spell out the details for how it will be used and run the risk of disagreement and other problems if they leave issues unaddressed.

2.3.1.2 Easements Implied in Subdivision

Sometimes an easement is created even though it is not mentioned in a deed or other recorded instrument. Most often this occurs with a subdivision. For example, an implied easement may arise if an owner of two lots installs a sewer line across one to serve another and then separately conveys the lots. Another common example is when an owner subdivides and one lot must be able to cross another for access to a road. Under such circumstances the obvious necessity of an easement may be seen as implying that the subdivider intended to reserve one despite not mentioning it in a recorded document. This is especially likely if the subdivider was actually using the real estate in this way before conveying one of the lots. However, when an easement is not clearly defined in a recorded instrument its existence remains uncertain until the parties reach an agreement or a court issues a decree.

Implied easements also can arise in a multi-lot subdivision according to a comprehensive plan of development. Conveyance of subdivided lots by reference to a recorded plan may be interpreted as implying rights shown on the plan and therefore apparently intended even though not expressly described in the deed for the lots. This is especially so when roads shown as part of a scheme of development are essential for reaching the public road. It may be logical to assume that the developer would not have intended to create lots without a way to get to the public road. Consequently, when deeds convey lots by reference to a plan showing roads, the conveyance may be deemed to have impliedly included easements for the lot owners' use of those streets.

Another circumstance that may suggest an easement was implied even though it was not described in a deed is actual use prior to a subdivision that seems to be an integral part of the new configuration. For example, an access route or other shared use may have become so well established and obvious that its continuance was obviously intended. This and the other examples illustrate that many questions can arise about easements and that their resolution usually depends on the particular circumstances.

2.3.1.3 Easements Created by Use

In rare circumstances easement rights can be acquired by one owner over another owner's land through actual use, without a recorded instrument, by what is called *prescription*. This can occur when someone continuously uses another's real estate for at least twenty years in an open way that equates to an obvious claim of a permanent right to do so. For example, a prescriptive claim could arise if the owner of one lot has used the other for continuous and obvious road access for many years. Essentially, the landowner whose real estate is being used is considered to have surrendered the right to object by waiting far too long to do so. Rights acquired by these means are not established by law until a court determines that all of the requirements for a prescriptive easement have been met. This means that either an agreement or litigation is necessary to settle the matter.

To create prescriptive rights, the use must be continuous in a manner that gives the landowner notice that the user seems to be claiming ownership. The kind of use that will be enough to show a claim is being made—called *adverse use*—depends on the nature of the real estate being used and the way it has been used. No one can acquire prescriptive rights merely by occasionally entering another person's real estate or by entering it secretively, such as to hunt or fish. Prescriptive rights cannot arise based on a use to which the claimant is otherwise entitled, such as a lease. Nor can prescriptive rights be obtained based on a use that occurred with the landowner's permission. If these were not the rules, landowners would risk losing their real estate merely by the neighborly act of allowing others to cross or use it. For example, the owner of a beach who voluntarily shares it with others as a friendly gesture, or who does not strictly enforce a boundary line against everyone at all times, is not at risk of losing the right to stop others' use. This notion of permissiveness is often the most difficult and disputed aspect of a claim of prescriptive rights.

Litigation about prescriptive rights usually arises when ownership changes and the owner of the land objects to continued use. The owner can bring legal action to prohibit continued use, or the claimant can bring an action for a court declaration of a right to continued use. The party claiming to have acquired an easement by prescription has the burden of proving that the use was by a claim of right rather than permissive.

2.3.1.4 Statutory Right to Cartways

The North Carolina statutes provide for an unusual procedure that enables a private landowner to use the eminent domain process to establish a private right-of-way at least eighteen feet wide over someone else's real estate to get to a public road if no private route is available. Known as the *cartway easement* procedure, the statute provides for a special proceeding in superior court to establish a "cartway, church road, mill road, or like easement."[5] The purposes for which a claim can be made include gaining access to land for cultivation, timber or mining operations, or industrial or manufacturing operations. In the court eminent domain procedure that must be followed, the landowner acquiring the easement right must pay the landowner for the right-of-way. The amount is based on the diminished fair market value of the subject real estate, which is equal to the difference between what the real estate was worth without the right-of-way and its value subject to the right-of-way, as determined by an appraisal.[6]

2.3.2 Scope of Easements

The rights and obligations of those involved with an easement are most clear when they have been fully described in a recorded deed or other recorded instrument and depicted on a recorded plat. Details minimize the possibility of disagreement about such things as the easement's precise location and dimensions, the conditions for its use, and the parties' obligations for maintenance. But even when an easement is created with precision and detail, disputes can arise. One reason for this is that easements are created within the context of land conditions existing at a particular point in time. As uses of the real estate evolve, and the real estate changes hands from owner to owner, questions or disagreements may arise by different people with different expectations about the extent of intended use and the parties' rights and obligations.

The general rule in determining the scope of an easement is to consider both what was originally intended and what is reasonable under the circumstances. Obviously this rule does not give any precise guidance about how any particular question will be resolved. Fortunately, those who are involved with an easement usually find their way to a reasonable accommodation of their interests. But occasionally one or the other party acts objectionably and court involvement becomes necessary to establish more clear rules.

When the rights and obligations involved with an easement are not defined in the document that created it, their scope will be construed according to the intent of the landowner who created the easement. For example, if the location and limits of a reserved right-of-way are not specified, a court will define the route as what would have been foreseen as

---

5. G.S. 136-68.
6. G.S. 136-68; G.S. 136-69.

reasonably necessary and convenient. A landowner's intent often can be seen in how the land is actually used. If the beneficiary of the easement first laid out the location and continued to use it without the landowner's objection, a reasonable conclusion can be drawn that the use is consistent with the landowner's original intent. Similarly, the beneficiary of a utility easement may have a right to continued maintenance of a line that was installed and has existed for some time if the landowner accepted it without objection.

Easement rights that are specifically mentioned in a recorded instrument may be useless without other, related implied rights. Implied rights may also carry obligations. For example, when an easement is for a right of access across a parcel, the beneficiary of that easement will likely have an implied right to keep the route free of obstructions. The landowner may in turn have an obligation not to alter the real estate configuration so as to make reasonable use of that right-of-way impossible. A rule of reasonableness also applies to the owner's right to continued use of the real estate subject to an easement.

The owner of real estate subject to an easement retains the right to use the land in ways that do not unreasonably interfere with the easement beneficiary's appropriate use. There is no simple rule for determining how the landowner and easement right owner's obligations and responsibilities are to be reconciled when they are not defined in a recorded instrument. For instance, unless prohibited in the instrument, the owner of the real estate may build structures within a right-of-way so long as they do not unreasonably interfere with the reasonable use by the holder of the right. Different people may have different ideas about what is reasonable, and disputes over use are usually resolved through compromise.

Landowners commonly misunderstand the scope of a utility easement. An instrument conveying an easement to a utility company is likely to include not only the right to install and maintain a line, but also a right to keep the line area cleared of trees, undergrowth, and structures. Someone may purchase real estate seeing only an unobtrusive utility line and not consider that the utility company may also have the right to enter real estate and clear it within the easement area. Owners are sometimes surprised to arrive at their land to see machinery or already cleared swaths of their real estate. Even if the instrument creating the easement was not very explicit about the rights to clear the real estate within the easement area, a right to do so may be deemed included as a reasonable part of the right to maintain the line.

The key consideration in determining the scope of an easement is what the owner who created it seems to have intended at the time. But the rights and obligations of those who come later are not necessarily frozen. The developer who created the easement is presumed to have anticipated some natural evolution in land use. What is reasonable depends on the particular circumstances. The question is whether any expanded use results in unreasonable conditions either for the owner to which the easement is subject or for others with rights to the easement. One of the most common disputes that arise in connection with an easement occurs when an owner who has an easement right looks to subdivide the benefited parcel or otherwise expand the use of the easement. For example, a party with the benefit of a cart path mentioned in a deed many years ago may look to subdivide and use the path for a roadway that will serve several lots. Or a utility that has the benefit of an easement for a line that serves a particular lot of real estate may want to use the easement to install a line that will serve other properties as well. The general rule is that the nature of permitted use may evolve to reflect changes in the way people travel and use real estate, if the change seems within what the original party who created the easement would have wanted. But the holder of an easement may not significantly increase the burden on the easement area, as is very likely to be the case if the attempted expansion is to serve multiple lots or lines or to create routes that have a significantly greater impact on the real estate.

2.3.3 Easement Termination

Most easements are intended to last indefinitely as part of a development scheme that benefits all who later own in the subdivision. They are said to run with the land, meaning they pass from owner to owner. Sometimes an easement is intended to be only temporary, such as when it is used only for access to a construction site or to use real estate for storing materials or equipment. Or it may be obtained by a business and last only so long as the business is operated. Under rare conditions the rights to an easement may terminate even though it was not created with a specified expiration date or event.

An easement may terminate if the easement beneficiary fully abandons its use. For example, this can happen if the owner of the lot over which the easement crosses has developed the lot in a way that indicates that the easement no longer serves any purpose and the party with the right to the easement has abandoned it use entirely for at least twenty years. A landowner claiming that an easement has been lost as a result of inconsistent development must show that the easement owner was aware of the situation and should have made known a claim to continued use. The erection of a fence or a gate does not necessarily prevent future use by the easement holder and, therefore, may not be enough to create circumstances in which the easement is deemed abandoned. On the other hand, if the landowner and easement beneficiary alter their use in such a way that the easement no longer serves any purpose, the easement may be deemed to have been modified or abandoned. For example, if adjoining landowners agreed to maintain a shared building entrance but changes are later made creating separate entrances without objection by either party, a court could determine that the restrictions regarding the common entrance were extinguished but that other aspects of the easement are still enforceable.

2.4 Restrictive Covenants

Real estate owners who subdivide their real estate often seek to restrict its use to create a neighborhood of compatible properties built according to a comprehensive plan. The goal can be as simple as ensuring that real estate is used only for residences or as complex as establishing detailed rules about construction arrangement and style. These requirements are a form of easement known as *restrictive covenants*. Most newly built communities, including lot subdivisions and condominiums, have extensive restrictive covenants.

The simplest case for enforcement of use restrictions is when the rules are carefully described in a recorded declaration for the subdivision. Each of the subdivided lot owners within the development would have the right to enforce the restrictions, including through litigation if necessary. Restrictive covenants can be enforced also by an association of homeowners within the protected community. The scope of covenants will be determined based on the circumstances at the time they were created and when they are sought to be enforced.

Restrictive covenants are subject to the same legal rules as easements about how they are created, how their scope is determined, and how they are terminated (discussed in Section 2.3). The details of how imprecise covenants are to be interpreted depend on the circumstances when the covenants were created and when they are sought to be enforced. In rare cases courts have found that covenants have become unenforceable because circumstances have changed so much that the restriction no longer serves a legitimate purpose. This is not likely to occur under modern conditions in which zoning restrictions and other regulations tend to preserve the character of neighborhoods.

2.5 Adverse Possession

Rightful ownership of real estate is almost always based on a deed or inheritance from a prior owner. Determining ownership is therefore almost always a matter of examining the real estate records at the register of deeds and probate files at the superior court. But there are cases in which ownership of land can be acquired based on actual use without a deed or inheritance, including the rarely applied doctrine known as *adverse possession*. In essence, adverse possession is a doctrine that requires an owner who can see that someone else is staking a claim to object within a reasonable time. By statute, in most cases no one may bring a lawsuit complaining about someone's claim as shown by actual use if the use has continued for at least twenty years.[7] The focus in determining whether ownership has been acquired by adverse possession is on the circumstances of the claimant's occupancy. For this to occur, the occupant must have made exclusive use of the real estate and it must have been obvious to the title owner.

Fencing in real estate and cutting trees may be clear evidence of occupancy and a claim of right. A claim of adverse possession may also be based on the long-time presence of a structure, as may occur when someone builds a garage over the line onto another owner's real estate. If for many years both owners act as if the boundary is according to the structure's location rather than according to record title, then the boundary as used may become permanent by adverse possession. Occasional use will not meet these requirements.

A claim based on adverse possession can occur even though ownership of the land has changed hands. Successive owners are able to add their periods of possession to meet the time requirement. Of course it becomes more difficult to prove that this has occurred when more than one owner is involved because evidence would have to be provided regarding each of the ownership periods.

---

7. G.S. 1-40.

The minimum period of occupancy required to acquire real estate by adverse possession is shortened from twenty to seven years when the real estate has been occupied "under known and visible boundaries under color of title."[8] "Color of title" refers to a recorded instrument that appears to have conveyed the real estate to the occupier but which for some reason was ineffective in doing so. The defective document on which a color of title is based can be a typical deed or a deed given at a foreclosure or as a result of sheriff's sale. For example, this may occur if someone acquired a deed believing it to be valid but the person who gave the deed did not have the title necessary for the conveyance or if the person who signed it did not have the legal capacity at the time due to some condition, such as young age. Even though the deed may not have transferred ownership, its recording may under the law be sufficient to put the actual owner on notice that the person occupying the real estate is claiming ownership.

A history of tax payments may be relevant, but it alone does not decide the adverse possession question. Of course people do not usually pay taxes on real estate they do not think they own, and hence payment of taxes may fairly be seen as implying a claim of ownership. However, the courts do not recognize payment of taxes as being enough to establish a valid claim of ownership over disputed real estate. Local government taxing authorities do not make a legal determination about title when they list someone as the owner for tax purposes; they are merely relying on the recorded instruments and presuming them to be valid. The North Carolina statutes provide that being listed as owner for tax purposes and paying the taxes raises a *presumption* of ownership for purposes of color of title under certain conditions even if the real estate has not been actually occupied. These additional conditions include occupying the land, marking boundaries, and recording a survey that refers to a recorded deed or other instrument.[9]

Title cannot be acquired in federal lands through adverse possession. North Carolina law also makes clear that no one can acquire title by adverse possession in any state or local government public road, alley, square, or other public way or in land in the public trust, such as watercourses and public beach access ways.[10] Title can be acquired by adverse possession in other land of the state government only with occupancy lasting at least thirty years or based on a recorded document under color

---

8. G.S. 1-38.

9. G.S. 1-38(b).

10. G.S. 1-45; G.S. 1-45.1.

of title for at least twenty-one years. The area of occupancy must be identifiable according to known and visible boundaries.[11]

Ownership rights cannot be acquired by adverse possession in a railroad right-of-way.[12] The law does not expect railroads to monitor the full length of their lines and object to those who might cross into it with their uses or structures. The statutes do provide that a claim can be made if the railroad has removed its tracks and abandoned the right-of-way for at least seven years, in which case ownership is presumed to go to the owners of adjacent parcels to the centerline of the abandoned easement, unless the origins of title show otherwise.[13]

2.6 Leases

The basic notion of a lease is obvious and well known: a tenant rents space from a landlord and pays rent. Almost all of us have had experience with a lease at some point in our lives. Despite their essential commonness, leases are governed by complex legal principles and rules. This section introduces some of these principles and rules.

Historically, giving someone a lease was considered to be a real estate conveyance, and as with other real estate transfers the parties were left to structure their arrangement as they saw fit. More recently, lawmakers have seen leases—especially for residential space—as something that should be restricted by law. Landlords and tenants still can structure relationships in many different ways to suit their agreement, but legislatures have imposed significant limitations on residential evictions and have provided tenants with tools to compel landlords to keep properties in fit condition.

Nothing formal or elaborate is necessary to create a legally enforceable lease. Short-term leases usually are not recorded in the register of deeds office. This is true of apartment rentals, which usually are one-year leases. When ownership changes hands for unrecorded leases, the lease likely will control whether the tenant's rights continue. But as described below, there are protections regarding a tenant's rights upon foreclosure of the landlord's real estate. By statute, only a lease for more than three years

---

11. G.S. 1-35.
12. G.S. 1-44.
13. G.S. 1-44.1; G.S. 1-44.2.

must be in writing.[14] Such a lease must be recorded with the register of deeds to take priority over the owner's later conveyances.[15] The recording is intended to give the tenant enforceable rights against buyers of the landlord's real estate and later lenders to whom the landlord gives mortgages. The recording can be done with a memorandum that states the basic terms, such as the parties and the term, rather than the complete lease.

A residential lease, especially for a unit in an apartment building, tends to be a form with which the particular landlord has become familiar and comfortable. Because leases must comply with state law and landlords compete for tenants, these kinds of leases tend to look very much alike. Commercial leases, on the other hand, usually are tailored to the circumstances of particular landlords, tenants, and leased real estate. In shopping centers and other multiuse properties, the leases have many of the same provisions but vary in other ways. For example, major chain stores that will anchor shopping centers have more leverage than small businesses occupying smaller spaces to get the terms that best fit their business plans.

2.6.1 Components of a Typical Lease

The following is a discussion of the primary issues addressed in a typical lease.

2.6.1.1 Parties

Leases will identify the landlord and the landlord's rights to transfer the lease rights to someone else upon a sale of the real estate. They will specify who the tenant is who is responsible for the rent and compliance with the other lease conditions; who else might be allowed to occupy the space, such as the tenant's family; and whether the tenant may transfer the rights or enter into a sublease with someone else for all or part of the space. A tenant may assign or sublease without the landlord's consent unless the lease prohibits it, but leases usually do prohibit it.[16] Unless the landlord and tenant agree, when an assignment or sublease occurs the original tenant remains responsible for the rent to the landlord.

Sometimes tenants find themselves with a change in landlord due to the landlord's business failure. If a landlord files for bankruptcy, the bankruptcy trustee has a defined time within which to accept the lease and

---

14. G.S. 22-2.
15. G.S. 47-18.
16. Smithfield Oil Co. v. Furlonge, 257 N.C. 388, 393, 126 S.E.2d 167, 171 (1962).

keep it in place or to reject it and take the space away from the tenant. The federal Bankruptcy Code gives tenants who file bankruptcy a right to assume and assign leases, provided that any defaults under the lease are cured by payment of past-due rent and adequate assurances are given of future performance.[17] This gives tenants a chance to catch up and either keep the space or find someone else to step in. The Bankruptcy Code invalidates lease clauses that provide that the lease is terminated if the tenant files for bankruptcy protection.[18]

2.6.1.2 Lease Premises and Common Areas

The leased space will be described either by reference to a unit that is clearly identifiable or with a real estate description. The lease also will describe what other real estate rights are included, such as parking or other areas devoted the tenant's exclusive use. The lease also will describe common areas for sharing among tenants, such as parking areas, common restrooms, elevators, utility rooms, and trash and loading areas. It will also specify the tenant's obligations in connection with use and maintenance of these areas.

A tenant has a right to occupy and quietly enjoy the premises. The right to occupy includes the right of reasonable use. In both residential and commercial leases a landlord can be deemed to have *evicted* a tenant when the landlord substantially interferes with the tenant's right of possession. An *actual eviction* occurs when the landlord physically excludes the tenant from the premises. An eviction can also be *constructive*, if the landlord has made the space so uninhabitable that the tenant rightfully abandons it, and if this occurs the tenant will no longer be responsible for the rent.[19] By statute the typical residential lease is assumed to include an implied warranty that the leased premises are suitable for occupancy.[20]

2.6.1.3 Permitted Use

The lease will describe the uses to which the tenant may put the premises. A residential lease will restrict use of the space to such purposes. A commercial lease will specify what the tenant may do. This component is especially important to commercial landlords because they want to prohibit

---

17. 11 U.S.C. § 365 (2006).

18. 11 U.S.C. § 365(e) (2006).

19. Marina Food Assocs., Inc. v. Marine Rest., Inc., 100 N.C. App. 82, 92, 394 S.E.2d 824, 830 (1990).

20. G.S. 42-42.

businesses on their property that would be harmful to other tenants or that interfere with rights granted to them for exclusive uses. Some commercial leases prohibit the landlord from allowing other tenants with competitive uses.

2.6.1.4 Term

Leases state the commencement and termination dates and any built-in options for extensions or renewals. Leases also specify any other applicable deadlines, such as dates for commencement of rental obligations, completion of construction, or occupancy.

2.6.1.5 Rent

Residential leases will specify the amount of the rent and the tenant's other financial responsibilities, such as payment of utilities or recreational space fees. This is usually a fixed amount per month, with a pro rata amount due for partial months. A typical commercial lease has a more complicated rent amount, including a *base* or *fixed* rent based on a market rate for each square foot of leased space, and *additional rent* for the tenant's share of expenses based on a relative percentage of leased space. Such expenses include common area maintenance, insurance, and real estate taxes. When the premises are to be used for retail sales or other businesses that rely on customer traffic, landlords may also negotiate for a *percentage rent*, which is a small fraction of the tenant's income after the tenant pays the rent.

Deadlines for payment of all rent components are set, usually the first of the month, in advance. Leases typically provide for interest or other penalties for late payments. Common area expenses and tax amounts are based on estimates using prior actual expenses, with provisions for reconciliation when actual expenses are determined. Tenants usually have a reasonable opportunity to audit the account for charges passed through to the tenant.

As described below, security deposits for residential leases are subject to statutory restrictions. The lease should describe how the deposits will be held in a way that complies with these restrictions. Commercial leases also address security deposits, but these are not subject to the same restrictions.

2.6.1.6 Insurance

Leases usually leave it to tenants to decide whether to get an insurance policy to protect their possessions and insure themselves against liability for harm to occupants or visitors. Commercial leases usually require tenants to maintain comprehensive insurance with an insurer and form of policy as approved by the landlord. Such a lease will also require that the tenant's policy name the landlord as an additional insured so that the landlord can apply insurance payments toward the cost of repairing the damage. In commercial leases landlords also may be required to maintain insurance, specifically fire and extended coverage insurance for the building and common areas, the cost of which may be passed on to tenants.

2.6.1.7 Construction and Improvements

A residential lease usually will require the landlord's prior approval for any changes to the leased space. Landlords tend to want to keep spaces uniform and ready for later tenants. To keep the units from falling into obsolescence or disrepair landlords will have a regular schedule for upgrades, such as painting and carpet and appliance replacement. A commercial lease usually is more complicated, specifying the landlord's and tenant's obligations regarding finish work in the interior space and its maintenance. Particular items of concern include responsibilities for installing and maintaining the heating, ventilation, and air-conditioning (HVAC) system, telephone and data connections, restrooms, accommodations necessary for access by those with disabilities, elevators, lighting, and sprinkler systems. The lease will define the tenant's discretion to make alterations and install signs as well as the process for obtaining any required landlord approval prior to making changes. The lease also will specify the parties' rights in what is installed in the space, such as lighting, shelves, and other fixtures.

2.6.1.8 Loss of Premises

The lease will describe what happens if all or part of the leased space is lost due to fire or government taking. The issues addressed in these provisions include the extent to which the space or the building in which it is contained must be affected before the tenant has the right to terminate the lease, the extent to which the landlord has the obligation to restore the premises, and what rights the tenant has to payment of eminent domain awards or insurance proceeds.

2.6.1.9 Default and Remedies

A residential lease normally will provide that the lease may be terminated if the tenant defaults by failing to pay rent, damaging the premises or allowing other occupants to damage them, or failing to comply with any other condition of the lease. To be enforceable, the remedies must be consistent with any applicable statutory mandates, as described below. The landlord's remedies will include the right but not the obligation to terminate the lease. Leases also may give each party a right to recover lawyers' fees for successful actions taken to enforce remedies against a defaulting party.

2.6.1.10 *Other Provisions*

Leases contain a variety of other provisions, some of which are common, and some of which are peculiar to the parties or the premises.

2.6.2 Statutory Mandates

The residential landlord–tenant relationship is affected by numerous statutory requirements. Manufactured housing park leases also are subject to extensive rules, which affect, among other things, landlords' control over tenants' conveyances, park management, facility charges, and grounds for eviction. Federal laws also may apply to leases, including commercial leases. For example, the Americans with Disabilities Act requires commercial facilities and public accommodations, as defined by the federal law, to remove existing architectural barriers to individuals with disabilities and to construct new facilities without them.[21] Both federal and state laws prohibit leasing discrimination on the basis of prohibited classifications. The number and extent of the various restrictions and obligations demonstrate how intensively the landlord–tenant relationship has become affected by governmental regulation; compliance requires vigilant attention to the always changing laws and regulations.

The most extensive rules in North Carolina apply to residential tenancies. By statute, residential landlords must comply with building codes, keep the premises in a fit and habitable condition, and keep common areas in a safe condition. Landlords must also promptly repair electrical, plumbing, sanitary, heating, ventilating, and air-conditioning systems when written notice is given by the tenant, except in emergency situations.[22] Smoke and carbon monoxide detectors also must be installed and maintained as specified by statute.[23] There are special provisions for penalties if residential landlords who are required to have smoke detectors or carbon monoxide detectors fail to do so.[24] Residential landlords must address

---

21. 42 U.S.C. §§ 12181–12189 (2006).
22. G.S. 42-42(a)(1)–(4).
23. G.S. 42-42(a)(5).
24. G.S. 42-44.

imminently dangerous conditions within a reasonable time. Such conditions include unsafe conditions involving wiring, flooring, steps, ceilings, roofs, chimneys, flues; lack of drinking water; no operable locks; broken windows; lack of operating heating systems, operable toilet or bathtub or shower; or the presence of rats due to structural defects. Landlords may charge tenants for repair of immediately dangerous conditions if the damage was the tenant's fault.[25]

The statutes limit the amount of late fees that a residential landlord may charge. Agreements for monthly rent may not charge more than 5 percent or $15 for a late fee, whichever is greater, with different amounts if rent is due in different installments. Landlords may include a fee of not more than the greater of 5 percent of monthly rent or $15 for having to file a complaint if the tenant cures the default and the landlord dismisses the action and not more than 10 percent of the monthly rent if the landlord succeeds in a small claims case for eviction. A landlord may not collect any late fee if the lease violates these limitations, even if the landlord's actual practice complied.[26]

Special statutory protections are given to tenants and their household members who are victims of domestic violence or stalking. Landlords may not terminate a tenancy or refuse to enter into one on the ground that the tenant or the tenant's household member has been a victim of domestic violence, sexual assault, or stalking.[27] Such a tenant has a right to have the locks changed at the tenant's expense within forty-eight hours if the landlord is given notice that a perpetrator of such crimes is not a tenant in the same unit and within seventy-two hours if the perpetrator is a resident of the same unit and the requesting tenant gives a copy of a court order instructing the perpetrator to stay away from the unit.[28] Such a tenant also has a statutory right to terminate a lease with thirty days' notice accompanied by an order or other documentation required by statute, in which case in general the tenant is not responsible for payment of rent after the early termination date. If other household members remain they become responsible under the lease.[29]

---

25. G.S. 42-42(a)(8).
26. G.S. 42-46.
27. G.S. 42-42.2.
28. G.S. 42-42.3.
29. G.S. 42-45.1.

A landlord may seek an order for immediate eviction if a tenant has been knowingly involved in drug dealing on the premises or had reason to know of it, subject to a defense based on certain actions the tenant has taken to prevent or report it.[30] Such an eviction order may be obtained in a small claims action, or by statute the landlord may bring an action for emergency relief in district court.[31]

Members of the armed forces who must move in connection with a permanent change of station or deployment have certain rights to terminate a lease.[32] Such a tenant is not liable for unpaid rent past the termination unless the tenant rented for less than nine months, in which case the statute limits the amount that can be charged, and additional termination rights apply in the event of death in service.[33] Members of the armed forces have certain rights in large rental facilities to terminate their leases if the real estate is foreclosed upon.[34]

A tenant may prevent an eviction if it is what is called "retaliatory" under the statute. An eviction is retaliatory if the tenant can show that the reason for the eviction is substantially because within the past year the tenant complained to the landlord about the landlord's failure to keep the premises in a fit condition as required by the statute, the tenant made a complaint about a health or safety law violation, the government issued a complaint to the landlord about the rented space, the tenant took action to enforce the lease or legal requirements that apply to it, or the tenant became involved with a tenants-rights group. These activities do not prevent a landlord from proceeding with the eviction if the tenant is not paying rent or complying with the lease, or the landlord has another good faith basis for the eviction as described in the statute.[35]

The N.C. State Fair Housing Act prohibits discrimination in real estate transactions and leasing on basis of race, color religion, sex, handicap condition, familial status, or national origin. In general the prohibitions and remedies apply to apartment buildings with four or more units.[36] Federal laws prohibit similar kinds of discrimination in projects funded through federal funds, and Title VIII of the Civil Rights Act of 1968 more generally

---

30. G.S. 42-64.
31. G.S. 42-68; G.S. 42-74.
32. G.S. 42-45.
33. G.S. 42-45(b).
34. G.S. 42-45.2.
35. G.S. 42-37.1.
36. G.S. Chapter 41A.

prohibits housing discrimination. Someone harmed by prohibited discrimination may complain to the N.C. Human Relations Commission.

The statutes impose requirements on tenants as well. They must keep their space in a clean and safe condition, comply with building and housing codes, and not deliberately or negligently damage the property. Tenants are also prohibited from disabling smoke or carbon monoxide detectors and must notify the landlord in writing if a detector needs to be repaired or replaced. They are responsible for all repairs made necessary by their deliberate or negligent actions other than ordinary wear and tear.[37]

2.6.3 Security Deposits

North Carolina statutes impose security deposit obligations on landlords of residential dwelling units other than single rooms.[38] Landlords for such properties may not require deposits of more than one and one-half months' rent for a monthly tenancy or two months' rent for longer terms.[39] Landlords must put security deposits in a North Carolina bank or savings institution, or furnish a bond in that amount from an insurance company. The landlord must notify the tenant of the location of the deposit within thirty days after the beginning of the lease term.[40] The statutes require landlords to give tenants notice when the landlord's interest is transferred, and unless the deposit is returned to the tenant the notice must give the name and address of the person to whom it has been transferred.[41]

The deposit may be used for nonpayment of rent; water or sewer charges under the lease; damage to the premises; costs of reletting, including broker fees; allowable charges for storing property left on the premises; allowed late and enforcement fees; and court costs.[42] When the lease ends the landlord must refund the deposit within thirty days or provide a list of what is being kept as damages. If a complete itemization cannot be completed, an interim accounting must be given within thirty days and a final within sixty. The statute provides that: "The landlord may not withhold as damages part of the security deposit for conditions that are due to normal wear and tear nor may the landlord retain an amount from the security

---

37. G.S. 42-43.
38. G.S. 42-56.
39. G.S. 42-51.
40. G.S. 42-50.
41. G.S. 42-54.
42. G.S. 42-51.

deposit which exceeds his actual damages."[43] Consequently, landlords who charge tenants for ordinary carpet cleaning or routine painting are violating the law, and tenants by statute may recover those amounts and their lawyers' fees for having to sue to recover them if the landlord's actions are found to have been willful.[44]

An additional reasonable amount may be required for pets.[45] It is not subject to the same restrictions as security deposits generally and need not be refundable.

2.6.4 Termination of Leases

A lease is terminated when the tenant no longer has the right to occupy the premises. This event can be by the actions of the parties, such as if the tenant gives the keys to the landlord and the landlord accepts them. Most leases expire after a year or a number of years, and no action of either party is necessary to end the tenant's occupancy rights on such a date. If the lease is to continue after the initial period set forth in the lease the landlord and tenant must agree to it, which often involves adjustments to the rent. Just as the parties' agreement or conduct can terminate a lease before its term expires, such action can also extend the lease beyond its termination date. In the absence of a specific extension, if a tenant remains the landlord has the option of beginning eviction or accepting rent. Accepting rent can result in a presumption that the landlord has agreed to a tenancy from year to year under the same conditions as the prior lease.[46]

By statute a residential tenant may terminate a lease when the space is destroyed or damaged so much that it is not reasonably fit for the purpose for which it was leased and the lease does not address making repairs. To invoke this right the tenant must give notice to the landlord within ten days of the damage.[47]

2.6.5 Landlord Actions to Regain Possession

A landlord cannot just physically remove a residential tenant for breach of the lease. The landlord must complete a court process to get the right to take possession. The statutes provide the landlord with a special procedure

---

43. G.S. 42-52.
44. G.S. 42-55.
45. G.S. 42-53.
46. Murrill v. Palmer, 164 N.C. 50, 54, 80 S.E. 55, 56 (1913).
47. G.S. 42-12.

for obtaining a judgment in court that takes less time than most litigation and is therefore called a *summary process*. The law also provides tenants with defenses based on landlord violations of their obligations and enables courts to permit tenants to remain in possession for a limited time under certain conditions.

Sometimes a landlord wants to terminate the lease before the expiration of the lease term for reasons related to the tenant's conduct. Most landlords include a provision in the lease called a *forfeiture* or *default* clause that specifies the tenant acts that give the landlord an option to terminate the lease. In addition to grounds for lease termination specified in the lease, the landlord may evict for criminal activity as described in Section 2.6.2.

If an eviction is for nonpayment of rent during a lease term, the landlord must give the tenant a notice insisting that either the rent be paid or the tenant leave the premises. This must be given at least ten days before an eviction action can be filed.[48] Tenants may stop the action by paying all the rent due as well as the landlord's costs of bringing the action.[49] A landlord also always has the right to evict a tenant who remains on the property after the lease has ended.[50] If the lease has a set expiration date and the date has passed, the landlord can file the action without further demand. If the lease does not have a set expiration date and is year to year, one month's notice is required; seven days is required for a month-to-month tenancy, and two days is enough for a week-to-week tenancy.[51] Manufactured home tenants must be given at least 60 days' notice and 180 days for a conversion to another use.[52]

After the required time has passed the landlord may file a *summary ejectment* case with the small claims court in the county. The superior court clerk has forms for such a case. The court then issues a summons that can be given to the sheriff for service of process. These documents will tell the tenant when and where the eviction court hearing will be. The summons will require the tenant to appear on a date not more than seven days from the issuance of the summons. The sheriff may serve the summons by mail or in person.

At the hearing, before a magistrate judge, the landlord must show that the tenant is in default or otherwise not entitled to the premises. If the

---

48. G.S. 42-3.
49. G.S. 42-33.
50. G.S. 42-26(a)(1).
51. G.S. 42-14.
52. G.S. 42-14; G.S. 42-14.3.

landlord wins the eviction case, the magistrate judge will award the landlord a *judgment for possession*. This is a court order that says the landlord is entitled to possession of the property and that the tenant has to vacate. The magistrate judge can also award a money judgment requiring the tenant to pay the landlord. The limit in the small claims eviction action is $5,000; if the landlord seeks a larger amount, a separate action will be required in district or superior court.[53]

The tenant will have ten days to appeal and have a hearing in district court. If the tenant does not appeal the magistrate judge's decision, or if the tenant loses the appeal, the tenant has to vacate within ten days. If the tenant does not vacate, then the landlord can ask the clerk of the court to enforce the judgment by issuing a *writ of possession*. The sheriff may then proceed to padlock the property and begin the procedure for allowing the tenant to remove personal property, as described in the following section.

2.6.6 Personal Property on Premises

Contrary to the popular impression, landlords are not automatically permitted to seize residential tenants' property and sell it to recover unpaid rent. North Carolina statutes impose obligations on the landlord to safeguard the tenant's property and to dispose of it only according to a prescribed procedure.

If a landlord obtains a writ of possession, property left on the premises worth no more than a small amount set by statute is deemed abandoned after five days, and the landlord may dispose of it. The sheriff will remove the personal property of an evicted tenant on the premises if the landlord pays the advance cost of its removal and storage for at least one month. If the property is worth more than the amount set by statute, the landlord must hold the property for at least ten days and give the tenant the opportunity to retrieve it. If the tenant does not retrieve it after ten days, the landlord may dispose of it, or may store it and sell it, giving the tenant at least one week's notice of the sale and the opportunity to retrieve the property if the tenant pays what is owed. If the tenant does not do so, the landlord may proceed with the sale and apply the proceeds to what is owed, with any surplus disbursed to the tenant upon request within ten days of the sale. If the property is worth less than a certain amount set by statute, the landlord may donate it to a nonprofit organization as long as the

---

53. G.S. 7A-210.

landlord gives the tenant notice this has been done and the organization first holds it for thirty days to enable the tenant to pick it up.[54] If a residential tenant dies and leaves property on the premises, there is a procedure the landlord can follow to sell it or give it to a nonprofit organization, after filing an affidavit in an approved form with the clerk of court and waiting a prescribed period determined by the value of the property.[55] Special rules apply to manufactured homes, including a lien by a landlord that survives for sixty days after the tenant vacates and may be enforced by public sale according to a statutory procedure.[56] Before proceeding with the disposal or sale of any property, landlords should check the details of current law.

2.6.7 Damages for Breach of Lease

Either party to a lease may suffer financial loss as a result of the other's breach of lease obligations, and damages for these losses may be available in court. A landlord's damages may include unpaid rent, losses from non-payment of rent owed for the remaining part of the term, costs to repair damage to the premises, and other costs incurred as a result of the tenant's breach of lease obligations.

In general, a landlord may recover all rental payments that have become due but were not paid by the tenant. Unless the landlord accepts a surrender of the premises, which terminates the tenant's obligations, a landlord may also recover unavoidable damages for rent that was to be paid for the remaining part of the term. The tenant may be liable to the landlord for the remaining rent, but the landlord must make reasonable efforts to minimize the loss by trying to find a substitute tenant. This is known as a *duty to mitigate.* If the landlord can with reasonable efforts rent to someone who pays the same or more rent, the landlord has not suffered damages from loss of rental income. If the landlord can only find a new tenant who will pay less, the recoverable damages would be the difference between this rent and the lease rent, provided the actual rent of the substitute tenant is reasonable. If the landlord does not make reasonable efforts to find a substitute tenant, the damages will be limited to the difference between the lease rent and the fair market rent that the landlord could have obtained with reasonable efforts.[57]

---

54. G.S. 42-25.9(d), (h).
55. G.S. 28A-25-1.2 (S.L. 2012-17).
56. G.S. 42-36.2.
57. Isbey v. Crews, 55 N.C. App. 47, 51, 284 S.E.2d 534, 537 (1981).

A tenant may recover rent paid if the landlord breached the lease or failed to meet the statutory obligations. In most cases, the amount recovered would be the difference between what was paid under the lease and the market value of the premises in its unsatisfactory condition.[58]

2.7 Planned Communities

The North Carolina statutes describe a method for a developer to subject a subdivision to restrictions and association governance according to rules for a planned community. Although any owners in a planned community may define their rights and obligations, the Planned Community Act overlays many aspects of how such features as roads and common areas are to be governed.

By statute, a subdivision with twenty or more lots, any of which are residential, created after January 1, 1999, is subject to the Planned Community Act. Some provisions of the act apply to subdivisions created before that date.[59] Planned communities that are not automatically subject to the statute may elect to abide by them. A planned community is formed when a declaration is recorded.[60] The community cannot be terminated except by agreement of at least 80 percent of the lots with votes, though the declaration can make the required percentage even higher.[61] Planned communities must have a homeowners association that has the power to own common areas, adopt bylaws and budgets, purchase insurance, hire managing agents, impose assessments to pay for common expenses, and carry out other powers to govern the community.[62] The bylaws may delegate many of the day-to-day decisions to an executive board.[63] The association must maintain property and liability insurance on the common areas if it is reasonably available.[64] The statutes authorize the association to invoke a lien on a lot if assessments remain unpaid for at least thirty days and a claim of the lien is filed with the clerk of superior court, and

---

58. Dean v. Hill, 171 N.C. App. 479, 486–87, 615 S.E.2d 699, 703 (2005).
59. G.S. 47F-1-102.
60. G.S. 47F-2-103(23).
61. G.S. 47F-2-118.
62. G.S. 47F-3-102.
63. G.S. 47F-3-103.
64. G.S. 47F-3-113.

this lien can be used within three years for a foreclosure according to the statutory procedure.[65]

The Planned Community Act also has limitations on the extent to which a community can regulate the display of flags and political signs. Among other things, the statute requires that any restrictions on displaying the U.S. or North Carolina flags must be described in the declaration in a prescribed, conspicuous way so that individuals have clear notice of the restrictions. The statute also limits the duration and nature of political sign restrictions and how such restrictions are to be included in the declaration.[66]

2.8 Condominiums

As land development has intensified, developers and real estate owners have sought creative arrangements for coordinating living spaces and subjecting them to community management. A commonly used technique to accomplish this is a condominium. Condominiums are subject to local and state regulatory requirements. They are subject to land use board scrutiny at the local level, which will include consideration of the descriptive information and plans. Public offering statements must be made available to potential purchasers of a residential condominium unit and must have required information, including descriptive information about the condominium and the association's budget.[67] By statute residential condominium buyers have seven calendar days to cancel a purchase contract after it has been signed.[68]

To create a condominium, a developer records with the register of deeds certain required documents that invoke rules in the state Condominium Act[69] and address variations in the details of how the units will be built and how they will share common facilities and responsibilities. The developer who creates and records these documents is known as a *declarant*. The master document is a *declaration of condominium*.[70] It provides detailed information about the boundaries of the land that will be part

---

65. G.S. 47F-3-116.
66. G.S. 47F-3-121.
67. G.S. 47C-4-102; G.S. 47C-4-103.
68. G.S. 47C-4-108.
69. G.S. Chapter 47C.
70. G.S. 47C-2-101.

of the condominium, the number and layout of the units, the *common areas*, such as roads, parking, recreational areas, and open space, and the percentage interest allocated to each unit. Portions of the common area dedicated to the exclusive use of one or more units, such as parking spaces, are known as *limited common area*. *Site plans* must show the boundaries and the footprints of the buildings and common areas.[71] *Floor plans* also are usually recorded to show the vertical and horizontal dimensions of the units. The statutes require that the declarant's plans show whether buildings or other depicted improvements must be built or need not be built.[72]

Details in the declaration and on the plans are important for understanding what it means to own a unit. Once these instruments have been recorded, each unit is a separate parcel of real estate for conveyance, mortgage, and taxation purposes. Once a condominium is created its layout and the rights and the obligations defined by the recorded instruments cannot be changed except by following the voting procedures set forth in the Condominium Act statute and the instruments. Except as allowed by the condominium instruments, unit owners may make changes within the unit only if they do not impair the unit's structural integrity, and they may not change the exterior appearance except as allowed by the instruments.[73]

The declarant initially controls and manages the operational details of a condominium, but these responsibilities pass to an association of the unit owners, which in turn is led by an executive board. The laws governing the extent to which a declarant may retain control are complicated. In general, a declarant may reserve a right to appoint and remove the members and officers of the association's executive board for up to two years after the earlier of when units are offered for sale or a right to add new units was last exercised, or 120 days after 75 percent of the units have been sold to someone other than the declarant.[74] These limits can be affected by a number of circumstances. Any reserved power will be stated in the declaration. The bylaws will describe the constitution and powers of a unit owner's owners' association to govern the common areas and manage common expenses and assessments. Associations elect an executive board comprised of at least three members, who will act in behalf of the association on routine

---

71. G.S. 47C-2-109(c).
72. G.S. 47C-2-109.
73. G.S. 47C-2-111.
74. G.S. 47C-3-103(d).

matters. The statutes prescribe certain requirements about its election and membership.

2.8.1 Common Problems Involving Condominiums

Condominiums can meet the desires of many for ownership within a designed community. They also involve common problems. A discussion of the most common follows.

2.8.1.1 Completion as Planned

Developers do not always build to match their plans and advertisements, especially when market conditions change after the project begins. Local land use regulators usually require developers to post bonds in case they do not complete improvements, but these are not always adequate to protect the unit buyers. Sometimes developers depart from their plans because they encounter obstacles or are just not paying attention, in which case unit owners may have conflicting rights, such as parking spaces that do not match the plans. Often these problems can be detected by careful review of the condominium instruments. Sometimes the association or individual owners must reach an agreement and undertake the procedures to amend the instruments. This can be costly.

2.8.1.2 Association Functioning

Condominiums involve shared rights and obligations, and many of these are managed by the association. The association is likely responsible for such ordinary things as common area maintenance, landscaping, and trash removal as well as insurance for the property. They also are likely to be responsible for major structural repairs that affect more than one unit. Carrying on these tasks effectively depends on a well-managed executive board and cooperative unit owners. Disputes are common among owners about appropriate action to take or not to take and how the costs should be shared, and such disputes sometimes result in litigation.

2.8.1.3 Assessment Collection

Unit owner associations levy assessments to their member owners for their share of common expenses for insurance, maintenance, repair, and replacement. This assessment is according to percentages specified in the condominium instruments. Some kinds of expenses are allocated to specific units. Unit owners sometimes fail to pay their assessments, and the association must then take action to collect. The association has authority to impose fines in amounts allowed by statute for assessments that remain unpaid for a certain time, and under certain circumstances an owner's privileges can be suspended. The association also may obtain a lien on which the association can foreclose using the same procedure followed for deeds of trust with a statutory power of sale. The association must follow a prescribed procedure to enforce the lien, including written notice in a form prescribed by the statute given to the owner at least fifteen days before the lien claim is filed with the county superior court. The lien will not take priority over deeds of trust already recorded; neither does it take precedence over taxes. If the proper procedure is followed, the association also can recover its costs and reasonable lawyers' fees for collecting unpaid assessments.[75]

2.8.1.4 Regulation Enforcement

The condominium's declaration and bylaws prescribe rules for use of the units and common areas. These may include rules for such things as pets, parking, noise, and signs as well as for changes to units' appearance. Many owners do not study these rules before they purchase, and others rent their units without telling their tenants about the rules. Some owners therefore violate the rules unintentionally, while others may do so intentionally but expecting that no one will complain. Enforcement of the rules can become difficult, especially if the action is not prompt or widespread violation has been tolerated. Problems can best be avoided if the rules are easily understood and consistently enforced.

2.8.1.5 Major Repairs

Condominiums involve structures and facilities that periodically require major repairs or replacement. They may also need unexpected repairs, such as to a failed roof, foundation, or mechanical system. Condominium budgets typically call for regular assessments to build a reserve fund to pay for these expenses as they arise. But unexpected expenses can require special assessments. Disputes can arise when owners have different views about the need for work or how it should be accomplished.

---

75. G.S. 47C-3-116.

2.9 Time Shares

A *time share* involves occupancy of a unit during five or more separated time periods over at least five years. Examples of time shares include vacation licenses, prepaid hotel reservations, and systems in which uses are awarded on the basis of points or vouchers.[76] The typical time share arrangement involves a transferrable right to exclusive occupancy of a unit during one or two weeks annually. Time shares involve considerations that are not associated with the typical ownership arrangement. They involve using the same space others use at different times of the year, and one person's misuse affects others' enjoyment. Time shares work best when effectively managed by a company that is able to handle fees, maintenance and cleaning, insurance, tax payments, and rule enforcement.

Consumer complaints about time shares commonly are based on misrepresentations in advertising. Many of these arise because time shares are bought through advertising or exchange programs without the kind of careful inspection and review undertaken by purchasers of other kinds of property. Those who are considering time shares may be able to detect deception by visiting the property, carefully inspecting the construction, and being sure to obtain and study information about how the project has been run and its operating budget.

Time share ownership can be shared the same as other real estate interests, such as in the form of tenants in common. Interests can be conveyed by contract, lease, or deed. By statute a developer is required to record an instrument showing conveyance of a time share interest. This must be done within forty-five days of the contract unless the developer establishes an account into which payments are deposited that complies with the statute, in which case the instrument can be recorded later.[77]

A developer must register a time share arrangement with the N.C. Real Estate Commission.[78] The developer also must provide potential buyers with a public offering statement that contains information about the property and notifies the buyer of a statutory right to cancel a purchase contract within five days of signing it.[79] Federal consumer protection and anti-fraud laws also apply to time shares, and they could be subject to state and federal securities regulations as well. The N.C. Real Estate Commission has

---

76. G.S. 93A-41(9).
77. G.S. 93A-42.
78. G.S. 93A-40.
79. G.S. 93A-44.

the power to suspend or revoke registration and to take other action if the developer violates the statute or engages in fraud or misrepresentation or other types of acts of misconduct listed in the statute.[80]

2.10 Life Estates

A *life estate* is an arrangement created with a deed by which someone receives property after someone else dies. The person who has a continued right during someone's lifetime, either the owner's or someone else's, is called a *life tenant*, and the person who gets the real estate after the death is called the *holder of a remainder* or *remainderman*. Once the life estate is created by delivery and recording of a deed, it cannot be reversed except with the cooperation of those who were given the remainder interest. Some lawyers and individuals use life estates to try to avoid having someone's estate go through a court probate proceeding after death. When a life estate has been created, the life estate ends and the real estate rights transfer automatically without need for probate.

People have sometimes used life estates for federal medical benefit eligibility purposes, to lower the value of someone's assets to qualify for assistance. Under some circumstances, for benefit eligibility purposes the real estate value is split, and the person retaining the life estate will not be considered as owning the entire real estate. This arrangement may not be effective in the short run, however, because there may be a look-back period under the law that counts real estate transferred within the previous several years. The full value of the house may be included in the estate for death tax purposes. Another common practice for those with substantial assets for the purpose of qualifying for benefits is a trust arrangement.

2.11 Trespass and Nuisance

The law has always provided a remedy for owners whose real estate is used without permission or legal authority, principally in the form of court orders to stop a trespass or nuisance. Impermissible or harmful activities that were once only addressed with the laws of trespass and nuisance are now addressed mostly through zoning laws and environmental regulations.

---

80. G.S. 93A-54.

But occasionally these forms of legal action still are used to address unauthorized or unreasonable real estate uses.

A *trespass* occurs when someone intentionally goes onto someone else's land without permission or other right to do so. This can be a one-time event, as when a protestor goes on private property and refuses to leave, or continuous action, such as when a structure is built on someone else's real estate. A trespass also occurs when someone enters another's real estate with permission but then stays longer than allowed.

Most commonly an issue of trespass arises when an owner asks law enforcement to remove someone who has entered without permission. Under state law, someone is guilty of trespass by entering into a building or onto real estate that has been enclosed in a way that demonstrates the owner's intent to keep people out, or by going onto land that has been posted with warnings to keep out.[81] Criminal penalties may apply depending on the nature of the real estate being entered.

Trespass sometimes also involves removing something from the land. The most common circumstances involving the removal of things from an estate are timbering, hunting, and fishing. Someone who damages or removes trees without permission knowing that the trees are on someone else's real estate is not only trespassing but also can be criminally prosecuted for larceny.[82] Trespass issues commonly arise with hunting and fishing. To hunt or fish on land that has been posted as no hunting or fishing by the landowner, the hunter of fisher must have written permission from the owner within the past year. Use of land leased to a hunting club is limited to someone carrying proof of membership in a club that has the owner's permission.[83] Someone who hunts or fishes on posted property can be prosecuted for a misdemeanor.[84] An owner may notify hunters that real estate is off limits by posting signs of a minimum dimension and at distances prescribed by statute—current laws should be checked.[85] Hunting and fishing are subject to many other state laws and regulations, and local laws may have more restrictions than these general state laws.

The issue of whether someone is trespassing also figures in the extent to which the owner can be responsible if the person is injured while on

---

81. G.S. 14-159.12; G.S. 14-159.13.
82. G.S. 14-135.
83. G.S. 14-159.6.
84. *Id.*
85. G.S. 14-159.7.

the real estate. The care that landowners owe to those who come on their land depends on the nature of the visit. To those who are invited onto the property landowners must exercise reasonable care to keep the property safe and warn of dangers. Landowners do not owe the same degree of care to trespassers. They may not intentionally hurt a trespasser by doing such things as leaving a known danger with the intent to do harm or being recklessly indifferent to whether someone is going to be hurt by a known danger.[86]

Something that is claimed to be a trespass sometimes is considered to be a nuisance under the law. In general, a *nuisance* is a very unreasonable land use. An activity becomes a nuisance as a result of its effect on its neighborhood. As the U.S. Supreme Court once put it, "A nuisance may be merely a right thing in the wrong place,—like a pig in the parlor instead of the barnyard."[87] For example, an activity that generates so much noise that it unreasonably interferes with others' reasonable uses of their own real estate could be a nuisance.

Something that might ordinarily not be a nuisance can become one through negligence. For example, if machinery is operated unreasonably it may become inappropriate for a neighborhood and constitute a nuisance. State and local environmental and public health officials can issue orders to stop a nuisance with respect to their fields of regulation,[88] and governments and their officials, as well as private citizens, may ask a court to order someone from continuing to create a nuisance.[89]

A landowner can be responsible for injuries caused by something called an *attractive nuisance*, which is a lure to children under circumstances in which the owner could have prevented the danger without ruining its usefulness. This doctrine does not apply to natural conditions that cannot be readily addressed, such as a flowing creek.[90]

Someone who suffers a loss as a result of a nuisance may be able to recover damages. Damages can include lost profits if the owner can prove with reasonable certainty that the harmful nuisance caused the loss. Damages for nuisance are difficult to prove, and courts do not allow speculative claims about decreases in value.

---

86. Jessup v. High Point, Thomasville, and Denton R.R., 244 N.C. 242, 245, 93 S.E.2d 84, 86 (1956).

87. Village of Euclid v. Ambler Realty Co., 272 U.S. 365, 388 (1926).

88. G.S. 130A-19.

89. G.S. 19-2.1.

90. Fitch v. Selwyn Vill., 234 N.C. 632, 634, 68 S.E.2d 255, 257 (1951).

3 Transfers

3.1 Overview

Real estate purchases are major events for both buyers and sellers. They involve a lot of money for all involved. For the buyer and seller, the mechanics of getting from an apparent agreement on the basics of a purchase to an actual closing may be puzzling. They usually rely on brokers, bankers, and lawyers and their assistants who handle many of these transactions and can anticipate what is needed to work through the details. These professionals have a sense of the complications that often arise and, if not handled well, can ruin the deal. This chapter is intended to give some insight into what can seem like a mysterious process for those who are not professionals. With a better understanding of the basic steps from agreement to closing, buyers and sellers can be better prepared to make the many decisions that must be made and to work with the professionals on both the routine matters and the unexpected.

The overall real estate purchase process can be understood within a framework of the milestones that usually occur. In a typical residential transaction, the following steps occur after a seller decides to offer the real estate for sale:

- The seller chooses and hires a broker and enters into a commission agreement, and the real estate and its listing price are advertised.
- The potential buyer in search of real estate contacts a broker to see the real estate.
- The buyer makes an offer, the seller provides a property condition disclosure, and the seller and the buyer exchange counteroffers through brokers, usually using a form that the broker working with the buyer provides, until an agreement is reached and a written contract is signed with contingencies for the buyer to try to arrange financing and perform investigations.
- The buyer applies and gets approval for financing that will meet the amount set as a contingency in the contract.
- The buyer gets a structure and pest inspection and notifies the seller of items that need to be repaired according to their contract, and the parties reach agreement on those repairs.
- The buyer arranges for a lawyer to do a title examination, issue title insurance, and handle the closing.
- The seller arranges for a lawyer to prepare a deed, which will be reviewed by the buyer's lawyer.
- The seller gets payoff information for the seller's existing mortgage loan from the lender.
- The buyer arranges for homeowner's insurance that will take effect at the closing.
- The buyer or a broker makes the arrangements to change over responsibility for the utilities.

- The lawyer or someone under the lawyer's supervision handling the closing computes the payment allocations and tax allocation and provides this information to the parties before the closing.
- At the closing the deed and deed of trust and other important documents are signed, the payments are arranged, and the keys to the property are turned over.
- The lawyer or someone under the lawyer's supervision records the deed and deed of trust and issues the title insurance policy.
- The seller's lender forwards the satisfaction document for the paid-off loan, either directly to the register of deeds or to the seller or to someone else who will deliver it to the register for recording.

Although commercial real estate sales involve the same basic steps, they also involve more elaborate negotiations and agreements about the real estate and activities on it, the kinds of information that will be disclosed, and other kinds of research into the real estate, such as environmental conditions and regulatory approvals, which are known as *due diligence* investigations.

3.2 Contracts and Conditions

When a buyer and seller agree on a sale they enter into a contract to define their rights and obligations. Most use a standard form supplied by a broker. The usual real estate purchase agreement contains standard terms and conditions that commit the buyer to a purchase but also enables the buyer to see if financing can be arranged and to do some investigation to ensure that the real estate is as advertised. The parties do not have to follow the standard form; that is their choice. Regardless of whether they negotiate specifics or just use a standard form, when they sign the contract they become bound by it and subject to legal liability on the terms on which they have agreed. The full contents of the contract should therefore be understood before signing.

3.2.1 General Requirements for an Enforceable Contract

Although in many circumstances parties can make an enforceable contract without a written agreement, either by orally agreeing or by simply beginning to take action based on the agreement, the law has long been that only in rare circumstances can a real estate contract exist without it being in writing. This is based on a centuries-old law derived from England called the Statute of Frauds. The North Carolina version of this statute provides that all contracts to sell or convey land and buildings, to lease for more than three years, or to lease land for minerals or mining must "be put in writing and signed by the party to be charged therewith, or by some other person by him thereto lawfully authorized."[1]

The statute of frauds requires that real estate conveyances be in writing, but not much is needed to satisfy this requirement. For example, the necessary written evidence of a contract may be contained within an exchange of letters. The statute does require that the document be signed by the party against whom it is to be enforced. A signature anywhere in the document indicating intent to be bound will suffice, but a printed or typed name is not sufficient unless other evidence indicates that this appearance of the name was intended as a signature, as could be the case with an email.

Of course the contract must identify the real estate. The boundaries need not be described in any particular way in the document to satisfy the statute of frauds. There just must be enough information to figure out what real estate is intended, which can be by reference to a street address or deed.

As noted above, only rarely can an oral agreement to convey real estate be enforceable by law. There have been cases involving fraud or breach of a trust agreement when courts have found that someone was obliged to transfer real estate despite the absence of a written agreement. Courts have the power to impose a trust on property and order it to be held or transferred according in the best interest of the person who was intended to have benefitted from it. A trust may be imposed, for example, if one person acquires real estate intending to hold it for the benefit of someone else who paid for it, as might occur in the context of a family or other relationship of special confidence. The proof of such an implied promise must be clear and convincing for it to be legally enforceable.[2]

Unlike most states, in general North Carolina does not recognize enforceability of an oral agreement for the conveyance of real estate based on part performance, such as part payment as might occur if a buyer gives a seller a deposit but there is no written contract. Even though an oral

---

1. Section 22-2 of the North Carolina General Statutes (hereinafter G.S.).
2. Wilson v. Williams, 215 N.C. 407, 411, 2 S.E.2d 19, 22 (1939).

agreement to purchase real estate is not enforceable in the sense that the seller can be compelled to convey the property, someone who has made advanced payment or has made improvements to the real estate may be legally entitled to payment for their value from the owner who accepted them, such as reimbursement if work was begun on the real estate.[3]

3.2.2 Required Building Condition Disclosures

Buyers should want to learn as much as possible about real estate before they buy it. This can be hard to remember amid the excitement of envisioning a new home and attending to a loan for its purchase. With care a lot of information can be learned by carefully looking at the property—not just cosmetic things, but also important features, such as roofs, foundations, drainage, heating and cooling, and appliances. Buyers can learn much more about the structure by having a professional inspection. Buyers therefore usually include in the contract the right to have inspections and to cancel the contract if major problems are uncovered. But even before the buyer makes a deposit and incurs the expenses of inspection, the buyer may expect the seller to share basic information about the property and serious problems with it. But contrary to what many may assume, the seller does not have a legal obligation to offer all information known about problems with the property. Under North Carolina law, a seller may choose either to complete the form by disclosing all known information on it or to indicate on the form the choice not to disclose.

North Carolina's Residential Property Disclosure Act requires sellers of residences to complete and provide a disclosure form to the buyer. Brokers typically provide sellers with the form, but it is required regardless of whether a broker is involved.[4] The requirement does not apply to court-ordered transfers, transfers by foreclosure sales, tax sales, or transfers to the government. It does not apply to transfers from a deceased person's estate or through a guardianship, conservatorship, or trust; between co-owners or spouses or as a result of a divorce; or to children or grandchildren. It does not apply to leases with an option to purchase if the tenant will be the occupant. Neither does it apply if the parties both agree not to complete it.[5]

---

3. Pickelsimer v. Pickelsimer, 257 N.C. 696, 699, 127 S.E.2d 557, 560 (1962).
4. G.S. 47E-1.
5. G.S. 47E-2.

To comply with the statute, the seller must provide the buyer with the completed form by the time an offer is made, thereby enabling the buyer to consider the information before making an offer that can be accepted.[6] It may be included in the purchase contract or as an addendum to it. The form provided by the N.C. Real Estate Commission lists the basic property features in which a buyer would ordinarily be interested. These features include water and sewer, roof, chimneys, floors, foundation, basement, plumbing, electrical, heating, and cooling. The form also calls for disclosure of information about pest infestation, land use restrictions affecting the real estate, and the presence of lead-based paint, asbestos, radon gas, methane gas, underground storage tanks, hazardous material, and other environmental contamination.

The seller may either indicate actual knowledge of these items or choose to state that the seller makes no representations about some or all of them.[7] The form merely says what the seller knows; it is not a guarantee that a problem does not exist. As described below, buyers typically hire an experienced inspector to check behind the seller's representations. A seller who chooses to make no representation will not be held liable for failing to provide known information on the form. By saying that no representation is made, the seller is in effect putting the buyer on notice to be especially diligent with inspections. By statute, a seller can satisfy the disclosure requirements also by giving the buyer a copy of a written report from a public agency or qualified expert that describes the condition of the features about which disclosure is required rather than attempt to describe it. In that case the seller will not be liable for errors in the report if the owner was not grossly negligent in obtaining the report or providing it.[8]

If the seller does not provide the form by the time of the offer, the buyer may cancel the contract within three calendar days after signing or within three days of receiving the disclosure if it is provided after the offer, unless the closing occurs sooner.[9] The seller has a continuing duty to provide further information if the seller discovers a material inaccuracy in what was represented, or the seller may instead choose to make the repairs necessary so that the information is not inaccurate. Reasonable wear and tear

---

6. G.S. 47E-5.
7. G.S. 47E-4.
8. G.S. 47E-6.
9. G.S. 47E-5.

is not a change that has to be reported.[10] There is no separate legal action for damages against a seller for failure to provide the form.[11] However, the seller could be liable for fraud or misrepresentation.

3.2.3 Deposit

The usual real estate contract requires the buyer to make an *earnest money deposit*, so-called because it is meant to prove the buyer's serious commitment to the purchase. When the parties enter into a contract, the seller will be relying on the buyer's promise and not be able to enter into an agreement with a different buyer even at a higher price. The seller also may be counting on the purchase payment for purchasing other property. In turn, the buyer is relying on the seller's promise, investing money in investigations and other preliminary steps, and expecting to own the real estate if the inspections and other conditions are satisfied. The deposit is therefore part of a serious commitment by both parties.

The amount of a deposit can vary widely and is a matter of the parties' agreement. A typical amount is several percentage points of the purchase price. As discussed below, the deposit usually is held by the broker, and this can create some unexpected dynamics. The amount of the deposit is important not only because it could be tied up during the contract period, but also because contracts usually provide that the seller may keep the deposit as *liquidated damages* if the buyer defaults (see Section 3.12.2.3). Of course a seller wants the deposit to be as large as possible to bind the buyer and as a potential remedy for a breach of contract, and the buyer wants it to be as low as possible so that money is not tied up in case the purchase becomes problematic.

3.2.4 Deadlines

Parties to real estate purchase contracts are often surprised to learn that not all deadlines within them are strictly enforceable. Much may depend on the chosen closing date, such as the time frame for getting financing and the seller's efforts to acquire and move into another place. Despite these realities, under the law failure to conform strictly to the closing date or other deadline in a purchase contract generally does not automatically mean the party who relied on this date will have a legal remedy if it is passed.

---

10. G.S. 47E-7.
11. Little v. Stogner, 162 N.C. App. 25, 33, 592 S.E.2d 5, 10–11 (2004).

A strict deadline is unlikely to be inferred in a contract that does not expressly state that compliance with it is essential. If a deadline is not stated in such a way as to indicate that time is of the essence, by law a party has a reasonable time to perform the step at hand. Determining what constitutes a *reasonable time* depends on the particular circumstances. If a deadline passes without one party doing what was supposed to be done, and the other party says nothing about it, the delay will not likely be seen as sufficient to be a breach of contract. In any circumstance involving a failure to meet a deadline, the parties' obligations will be assessed within the context of the circumstances as they play out. To avoid any surprises, someone to whom a particular deadline is important should clearly state in the contract that it is a strict deadline and the parties agree that there should be a legal remedy for losses if it is not met.

3.2.5 Conditions

Buyers who must obtain financing or sell other real estate before being able to close on a purchase should identify such matters in the agreement with the seller as *conditions* to their obligation to purchase. Sellers also should spell out any conditions to their obligation to convey, such as being able to find a different property to purchase. If a circumstance arises in which someone is not able to meet a condition, the party for whose benefit the condition is set should promptly decide whether to invoke a remedy, such as terminate the contract. Failure to act can be deemed a *waiver* of the condition. A party who waives a condition no longer has the right to terminate the contract on the basis that the condition was not met. For example, a requirement that notice be given by the buyer of an inability to obtain financing by a certain time may be waived if the buyer lets the deadline pass without saying anything about it.

Among the most common subjects of conditions to the buyer's obligation to close are title, financing, and structural inspections. Following are descriptions of the most common features of these conditions.

3.2.5.1 *Title*

Buyers want to be sure that they are purchasing the real estate from the person who really owns it. They also do not want to find out later that someone else claims to have rights to the real estate to which the buyer did not agree, such as a right to use it for a utility line or a right-of-way. They therefore have two concerns regarding title: first, getting the sellers' assurance about no known problems; second, the ability to have a lawyer examine the title to the real estate and to withdraw from the agreement if research uncovers a serious problem.

The usual residential purchase contract requires the seller to deliver title with a general warranty deed conveying *fee simple marketable and insurance title* free of encumbrances except taxes that are to yet due, specifically identified liens or easements to which the buyer agrees, and utility easements and restrictive covenants that do not materially affect the value of the real estate. The contract also will specify that the real estate must have legal access to a public right-of-way. These requirements enable the buyer to terminate the contract and get the deposit back if an investigation shows that title cannot be delivered as promised. A requirement that the seller be able to deliver *marketable* title means "title that is free from major defect, such as a judgment or lien, and can be freely conveyed to a reasonable buyer."[12] There can be reasonable disagreement about what constitutes a major defect. Some problems clearly are major and make a title unmarketable, such as a deed from a prior owner that gives someone other than the seller an apparent claim to ownership or a recorded deed of trust that was not disclosed and may still be enforceable against the real estate. Other discrepancies seem obviously minor because they can be easily remedied, such as the absence of a record of satisfaction for a deed of trust that was paid off to a bank still in operation. But, by definition, marketability depends on what is considered a reasonable doubt, and this is susceptible to different opinions.

The usual contract condition that title be marketable is not a requirement that the real estate must have any minimum market value. The parties are free to agree on a price they think reasonable, and the law does not imply that it be at the market price. Some form contracts contain a condition that the buyer be able to obtain an appraisal showing the market value to be at least equal to the purchase price. This may be included because a lender requires it as a condition for full financing based on the purchase price. Sellers should understand that this condition means they are foregoing the free market option of having a buyer pay more than the real estate is worth.

Another title condition often used in a purchase contract is a requirement of *insurable title*. As explained below, with title insurance an institutional insurer provides certain assurances that the real estate described

---

12. Kniep v. Templeton, 185 N.C. App. 622, 633, 649 S.E.2d 425, 432 (2007).

in the policy is as it is described. Theoretically, any real estate is insurable at a certain price and subject to limitations required by the insurer. Title insurers may be willing to accept the risk of a potential problem that the buyer would rather not have. Consequently, use of the term insurable title without more detail may not do much to define what the parties mean by acceptable title.

3.2.5.2 *Financing*

Almost all real estate purchases are financed with a mortgage loan. As described in Chapter 4, in almost every case the lender will not close the loan without analyzing the borrower's credit and comparing the purchase price to the loan amount and the real estate's appraised value. Accordingly, a buyer will not be assured of loan availability until a few weeks after the contract terms are set. To address this risk purchase contracts usually have a *financing contingency* provision that gives the buyer a few weeks to apply for mortgage financing at a specified minimum term and maximum interest rate before the buyer is irrevocably committed to the closing.

Although economic realities necessitate that most sellers agree to include a financing contingency, the seller has legitimate concerns about the fact that the contract depends on the buyer's effort in getting that financing. The seller may want some assurance that the buyer will not use this contingency to get out of the contract for reasons unrelated to financing. To address this concern contracts usually require that the buyer apply for financing and provide the seller with notice by a certain date about whether it can been arranged. To protect sellers in situations where there is reasonable concern about the buyer's ability to obtain financing, sellers, usually at their brokers' suggestion, may also request buyers to provide what is called a *pre-qualification letter*. As discussed in Chapter 4, this is merely a calculation provided by a lender based on numbers given by the buyer and does not provide assurance that the lender will actually make the loan after investigating the relevant data.

A financing contingency is satisfied when the buyer gets a commitment for a loan from a lender that meets the requirements stated in the purchase agreement. Once such a commitment is received it is as if the contingency did not exist; the buyer cannot terminate the contract merely by deciding not to go forward with the loan. The financing obtained need not match exactly the terms described in the contingency unless the contract says so. More commonly the contract requires only that the buyer be able to obtain a loan of at least a minimum amount at a rate not higher than a reasonable maximum based on current market rates. If something happens beyond the buyer's control to cause the financing to be withdrawn, the parties are left to work together toward a closing. The parties' obligations in this situation are not entirely clear. To meet legal obligations the buyer would most likely be expected to reapply for financing as soon as reasonably possible, and absent special circumstances, the seller would be expected to provide a reasonable extension to allow that to happen.

3.2.5.3 Structural Inspections

Buyers usually choose a property based on first impressions. Cosmetic issues, such as a need to paint or upgrade appliances, are expected and generally factored into the price being offered. But even if buyers take their time to look carefully for items that may be in need of repair, they are unlikely to have the expertise to detect problems that lie below the surface, such as faulty foundations, leaky roofs, mold infestation, or failing heating or air-conditioning units. To enable buyers to learn more about the possibility of major building problems and their impact on a fair price, buyers can insist on an inspection contingency in the contact, and they almost always do.

As described in Section 3.2.2, North Carolina law requires residential real estate sellers to provide a disclosure form that either gives information about the real estate or states that the seller is not going to provide such information. In addition to this form, the buyer can negotiate specific assurances from the seller in the contract. The most commonly used form of residential purchase contract contains a condition that certain features of the structure will be "performing the function for which intended" and "not be in need of immediate repair" unless specifically listed as an exception. Among the features usually included are built-in appliances, water, sewer, electrical, plumbing, heating, and cooling systems, roof coverings, doors and windows, exterior building surfaces, foundations, retaining walls, columns, chimneys, floors, walls, ceilings, roofs, porches and decks, fireplaces and flues, crawl space, and attic ventilation systems. An additional common condition is that there are to be no unusual drainage conditions or evidence of excessive moisture and no asbestos or other contamination at the property.

To enable the buyer to verify these conditions the contract gives the buyer the opportunity to get professional inspections and to give written notice by a certain date of any necessary repairs. If the buyer decides not to inspect or fails to do so by the deadline, the condition will be waived and the buyer will have to take the property as it is. If the inspection reveals conditions that the contract prohibits, and the buyer must give notice of required repairs by the deadline, the seller then has several options. The seller may make the repairs by a specified date. Or the seller may give the buyer notice that some or all of the repairs will not be made, in which case the buyer can either go forward without the repairs that the seller refuses to make or terminate the contract and get the deposit back. Or, as is often the case, the buyer and seller negotiate a compromise with some of the repairs being made and perhaps with an adjustment to the contract price for those that are not.

The standard contract also gives the buyer a number of other inspection rights. The buyer may get an inspection for wood-destroying insects and give the same kind of notice as is given for the general home inspection. Also, buyers typically have the right to check radon levels and to require the seller to fix the problem if the level exceeds U.S. Environmental Protection Agency acceptable limits. Radon is a naturally occurring gas linked to cancer that can penetrate structures from the ground and is not detectible without a test. The test, which involves exposing a material to the air and sending it to a laboratory for measurement, is relatively inexpensive. If excessive radon levels are detected, the problem sometimes can be addressed with ventilation changes.

The typical contract also has a condition that a buyer may terminate it if the estimated cost of repairs exceeds a certain amount without the buyer having to offer the seller the opportunity to make repairs. This clause can be the subject of serious disagreement due to the possibilities of disagreement about whether repairs are truly required and what a fair estimate of their cost should be. The contract also will provide that after the inspection, notice, and repair rights have either been exercised or the deadlines have passed without required action by the buyer, the property is deemed accepted in its "as is" condition.

Home inspection conditions often result in dispute. The buyer needs some ability to look carefully at the property before committing, and the buyer's mortgage lender will want assurances that it is worth what the buyer thinks it is worth. On the other hand, the seller needs some assurance that the price on which the parties agreed is for real and not just bait that the buyer will use to renegotiate based on a list of observations about property conditions that every buyer should reasonably expect to find. The process works best when the parties are realistic and reasonable. The home inspection condition should protect the buyer from being tied to a price that did not account for a newly discovered serious issue, such as a leaking roof, faulty foundation, or failed heating or cooling system. But it should not give the buyer the right to attempt to cancel the contract or renegotiate the price based on matters of preference or minor items attributable to normal wear and tear. These are things that should have been taken into account when the buyer made the offer. Brokers can be useful intermediaries to inform the parties about what is customary and perceived as fair.

The commonly used form of purchase contract also provides another alternative to the usual inspection process. With this option the buyer pays a nonrefundable fee for the right to have the property inspected and then to decide whether to terminate for any reason. In essence, the seller receives some compensation for taking the property off the market while the buyer decides whether to go forward. Estimating the appropriate amount of compensation can be difficult, and sellers usually are not inclined to agree to remove the property from the market with no real commitment by the buyer. This kind of option arrangement is more likely to be just a step toward renegotiation.

3.3 Brokers

No law requires someone to hire a broker to sell or buy real estate. But brokers play a prominent role in the real estate market. A national broker association has more than one million members; about nine out of ten home sales involve a broker.[13] Notwithstanding brokers' heavy involvement in real estate transactions, few people who pay brokers' commissions understand what a broker is legally required to do and what a broker is legally prohibited from doing.

When most people think of a broker, they think of someone an owner hires to advertise and sell a property. Usually a broker receives substantial compensation out of what is paid to the seller. This perspective of a broker as someone hired by a seller is the basic framework for the laws and regulations that govern brokers' conduct. Most brokers who receive commissions work for sellers and are paid by them, even when they deal with buyers. These arrangements can be confusing to those rarely involved in a home sale, and many of the laws and regulations governing brokers are

---

13. National Association of Realtors, Field Guide to Quick Real Estate Statistics (Nov. 2011), *available at* www.realtor.org/library/library/fg006.

aimed at preventing brokers from taking advantage of this confusion. This section introduces the basics of these laws and regulations.

3.3.1 Broker Regulation

Under North Carolina law, the person licensed to represent others in the sale or purchase of real estate is called a *broker,* who in some states can go by another name, such as *salesperson.* North Carolina statutes define a real estate broker as any person, association, or entity that offers to sell or buy, auctions, or negotiates to sell, exchange, or lease real estate.[14] This does not include those who engage in these activities as lawyers or trustees or who sell their own property.[15] Brokers are sometimes called *real estate agents,* which obviously refers to the fact that brokers deal with real estate for someone else's account. The word *Realtor* also is used to describe brokers in general, but the term is a registered trademark that identifies a member of the National Association of Realtors. In this chapter, those involved in brokerage activities are generally referred to as brokers.

In North Carolina, by statute, no one may "act as a real estate broker, or directly or indirectly . . . engage or assume to engage in the business of real estate broker or to advertise or hold himself or herself or themselves out as engaging in or conducting such business without first obtaining a license issued by the North Carolina Real Estate Commission."[16] Someone can act as a broker in North Carolina only after taking a pre-licensing course and passing an examination given by the N.C. Real Estate Commission. Such a person is initially called a *provisional broker* and must be supervised by a person who qualifies as a *broker-in-charge.* To be a broker-in-charge, a person must have two years of experience and complete a course of instruction. Provisional brokers must complete a required post-licensing education course within three years to become a broker.

Brokers are subject to North Carolina state laws and the regulations of the N.C. Real Estate Commission. Among other things, the commission's rules have education and examination requirements for broker and salesperson licensing, rules about broker interactions with clients and each other, and procedures for complaints, hearings, and disciplinary action.

---

14. G.S. 93A-2(a).
15. G.S. 93A-2(c).
16. G.S. 93A-1.

The commission also has the power to bring legal action to stop an unlicensed person from engaging in broker activities.[17]

The statutes contain a list of improper acts that could become the basis for suspension or revocation of a broker's license, including making misrepresentations of material facts, giving false advertisement or promises, failing to disclose agency relationships, failing to keep separate and account for others' money, failing to deliver documents as required, making prohibited payments to others, or engaging in other improper, fraudulent, or dishonest dealing.[18] The commission reviews complaints from clients and may investigate the allegations and conduct disciplinary hearings.

The N.C. Real Estate Commission rules require that brokers have a written agreement for their services. An agreement with an owner must be documented when the relationship is formed, and for a buyer or tenant the agreement must be signed not later than when an offer to purchase or rent is made, unless it is for a specified time, in which case it must be in place when the arrangement begins.[19]

3.3.2 Broker Roles

Brokers generally are seen as a valuable source of information about real estate because of their knowledge of properties for sale in a community. Rather than driving around neighborhoods and combing through advertisements, those looking to buy can visit a broker for a short list of properties with preferred characteristics. A buyer's broker can provide information about properties on the market and may also be aware of properties soon to become available, potentially giving the buyer an advantage compared to other buyers. With the ready availability of information about real estate on the Internet, including *for sale* listings and detailed valuation statistics from the tax assessor and other sources, potential buyers now can see for themselves much of the information that only brokers once seemed able to provide. But capable brokers are still commonly seen as well positioned to collect and distill relevant information and provide guidance about the contracting, financing, and closing procedures, especially to those who have no experience with real estate transactions.

---

17. G.S. 93A-6(a), (c).
18. G.S. 93A-6(a).
19. N.C. Admin Code (hereinafter N.C.A.C.) tit. 21, ch. 58A., § 0104(a) (2012).

Brokers' education, experience, and ethical standards vary widely. An experienced, knowledgeable, and honest broker can be valuable to a seller or a buyer. At the other end of the spectrum, some individuals who offer broker services have little special knowledge and may not have the skills or means to market a property effectively. Some do little more than put up a sign, submit information to a listing service, and wait for a buyer and commission to appear, which may pass without objection in a market in which homes sell quickly for asking prices.

Both the seller and the buyer should remember that the dynamics of a real estate transaction are such that a broker wants a sale and often receives a large commission. A slightly higher sale price may be important to a seller but of relatively little economic value to a broker, who prefers to close a deal, collect a commission, and move onto another possible sale. Even worse, a rare broker may be willing to walk close to the line of illegal or unethical conduct, or cross right over it, to get a large commission.

Increasingly brokers have sought to expand their services to include referrals to lenders, home warranty companies, home inspectors, and closing lawyers. Recognizing that sellers and buyers generally do not understand the value of services offered in connection with home sale, federal and state laws restrict many kinds of broker activities and require disclosures in connection with others. For example, federal law prohibits anyone from giving or accepting a kickback in exchange for referrals of settlement service business involving a federally related mortgage loan, which applies to most loans.[20] Settlement services for which referral fees may not be paid include title searches and other lawyer services, closing services, title insurance, surveys, appraisals, credit reports, home warranties, and inspections.[21] This does not prohibit brokers from identifying companies or individuals with whom they have had good experiences if no referral fee is involved, and it is not uncommon for professionals in the same industry to refer customers to each other as a professional courtesy. Some brokers interpret the restrictions as not prohibiting them from earning referral fees in connection with a business they do not consider to be a "settlement service," such as a company that performs repairs on structures. In any event, a buyer should independently consider the need for a service and the reputation of the person who will be performing it.

---

20. 12 U.S.C. § 2607 (2006).
21. 12 U.S.C. § 2602(3) (2006).

3.3.3 Agency Relationships

Brokers act as agents, and the law gives them certain kinds of authority for their clients and restricts how they can deal with others. Brokers do not have any authority to sell or buy property for clients unless they specifically give that authority. Except in rare circumstances brokers' statements that their clients are willing to enter into agreements do not bind their clients until the buyer and seller sign a contract with each other.

As an agent, a broker owes what the law calls a *fiduciary duty* to the broker's client. Simply put, a fiduciary duty means the broker must act in the client's best interest. Under the law the client is known as a *principal*. As the N.C. Court of Appeals said, this "very relation implies that the principal has placed trust or confidence in the agent, and the agent or employee is bound to the exercise of the utmost good faith, loyalty, and honesty toward his principal or employer."[22] A broker who is representing a seller must strive to maximize the seller's price and other interests. This means, for example, that a broker cannot make a decision to the seller's disadvantage, such as pressuring the seller to take a lower price because the broker wants quicker sales to maximize commissions.

In most transactions at least one and probably two brokers are agents *for the seller*. The *listing broker* will be the person whom the seller hires to advertise the property and bring a ready, willing, and able buyer. This broker usually has authority in the agreement with the seller to offer to share a commission with other brokers who bring a buyer to the property. Probably the most common misconception about loyalties occurs when a buyer contacts a broker about a property offered through a multiple listing service, as usually is the case. Multiple listing services enable brokers across the country to advertise properties and offer to share their commissions with a cooperating broker who brings a buyer. The buyer's initial contact is with the cooperating broker, who may never have met the seller, which can give the buyer the wrong impression that the cooperating broker is the buyer's agent. The cooperating broker will receive part of the commission paid by the seller and should properly be viewed as the seller's subagent, not as a buyer's agent or a dual agent of both the seller and the buyer.

In North Carolina, a broker is required to present the brochure *Working with Real Estate Agents* to a prospective buyer or seller at the first substantial contact when the consumer or broker begins to act as though an agency relationship exists and the consumer begins to disclose personal or

---

22. SNML Corp. v. Bank of N.C., 41 N.C. App. 28, 37, 254 S.E.2d 274, 280 (1979).

confidential information to the broker. It contains the following information (the emphasized words are as they appear):

Seller's Agent Working with a Buyer

If the real estate agent or firm that you contact does not offer *buyer agency* or you do not want them to act as your *buyer agent*, you can still work with the firm and its agents. However, they will be acting as the *seller's agent* (or "subagent"). The agent can still help you find and purchase property and provide many of the same services as a *buyer's agent*. The agent must be fair with you and provide you with any "material facts" (such as a leaky roof) about properties.

But remember, the agent represents the seller—not you—and therefore must try to obtain for the seller the best possible price and terms for the seller's property. Furthermore, a *seller's agent* is required to give the seller any information about you (even personal, financial or confidential information) that would help the seller in the sale of his or her real estate. Agents must tell you *in writing* if they are *sellers' agents* before you say anything that can help the seller. But until you are sure that an agent is not a *seller's agent*, you should avoid saying anything you do *not* want a seller to know.

Buyers who are handed this brochure at their first visit to a home may not take the time to read it and may have difficulty understanding what it means. Even buyers who carefully read this advice can easily forget about it when they get involved in buying the home. Their assumptions may be different from what is explained in the brochure. Commonly buyers are making the direct contact and meeting with a broker alone, and it is hard to remember that the broker may actually represent the seller. Buyers should keep in mind the broker's real loyalties. This means, for example, that a buyer who makes an offer with a listing or cooperating broker should not disclose a readiness to pay even more, because that broker aims to maximize the seller's price. Similarly, buyers should not reveal that they are committed to purchasing the property unless they are willing to forego the bargaining leverage that comes with demonstrating a willingness to walk away.

Buyers and sellers may be surprised that the law allows a broker to be what is called a *dual agent* for both the seller and buyer in the same transaction. Such an arrangement seems logically inconsistent with the notion that brokers are acting in the best interest of their clients because no one can simultaneously represent the best interests of someone seeking to maximize a price and someone seeking to minimize a price. As the N.C. Supreme Court once observed, "a man cannot be the agent of both the buyer and seller in the same transaction, without the intelligent consent of both parties."[23] However, the N.C. Real Estate Commission's regulations allow a broker to represent more than one party in a transaction if each of the parties gives written approval.[24] A brokerage firm may represent both the buyer and seller in the same transaction by assigning individual brokers to each party. This can only be done with prior written approval from both clients, and no broker may undertake to represent a party in the same transaction after already receiving confidential information from the other party.[25] The Real Estate Commission's rules note that the agreement for dual representation may expressly provide that the broker is not to disclose information received from one party to the other party about a willingness to vary the price from what is offered, the motivation for the transaction, or other confidential information. Some states prohibit dual agents from ever doing this; North Carolina leaves it up to the client. Even with these written promises, the parties should consider if they can be satisfied that the broker will be able to act and make recommendations with the kind of loyalty that the parties expect.

3.3.4 Commissions

Usually a broker's right to a commission is clearly defined in a contract between the broker and the client and there is no disagreement about payment. The commission becomes an item on the closing settlement statement, and the deposit is released to the broker to pay it, together with any additional amount needed from the closing proceeds to equal the full amount. But as described above, broker relationships can be confusing and parties may have different perspectives about the extent to which a broker brought about a sale and is entitled to a commission. Sometimes uncertainty or disagreement arises about whether a broker is entitled to a commission or a share of a commission. The following describes how the law tries to address the unclear situations.

In the typical *exclusive listing agreement*, the seller agrees to have the broker market the property at a set listing price and to pay a commission

---

23. Vinson v. Pugh, 173 N.C. 189, 194, 91 S.E. 838, 840 (1917) (quoting Ferguson v. Gooch, 265 S.E. 397, 399–400 (Va. 1896)).
24. 21 N.C.A.C. 58A .0104(d).
25. 21 N.C.A.C. 58A .0404(j).

if anyone buys the property while the agreement is in effect, for a period such as three or six months. The seller agrees to pay a commission if the broker presents a buyer who is ready, willing, and able to purchase at the listing price or at another price agreeable to the seller. The seller also promises not to deal directly with any interested buyer during the agreement and instead to refer such individuals to the broker. With this type of arrangement, the seller is committing to having only the broker find a buyer. This arrangement gives the broker incentive to find a buyer because the broker is assured of payment if there is a closing. But a seller may not be happy with paying a commission if the broker really had nothing to do with finding the buyer.

In an *open listing agreement*, the seller agrees to pay a broker *only* if the broker procures a ready, willing, and able buyer at the seller's listing price or at another price to which the seller agrees. In this type of agreement the seller is left free to hire another agent or to sell the property without a broker. This type of arrangement can create difficulty in determining when a commission is owed. For example, if a seller agrees to sell the property to someone with whom a broker has already dealt, but the seller was unaware that this contact happened, the broker may have a claim to a commission and the seller may not have taken the commission into account when assessing the price that is being offered. One way to attempt to avoid problems with this arrangement is to require the broker to notify the seller at the end of the agency agreement about everyone with whom the broker has communicated as a potential buyer and also to specify the extent to which a commission would be owed if a deal is reached with a listed potential buyer.

How long a broker has to earn a commission is another area of potential dispute. Commission agreements usually have a defined term—six months is typical. But unless the agreement clearly defines what happens after the term expires, there can be disagreement. Typically, the agreement requires payment of a commission if the property is sold within ninety days, or within another defined period, to someone whom the broker introduced to the seller during the agreement's term. To avoid confusion, agreements can require brokers to identify all prospective buyers with whom they have dealt, so that if sales occur to others, or if the notice is not given, no commission is owed. The typical agency agreement also provides that within a certain number of days after the listing period ends the broker may provide the seller with a list of persons whose attention was called to the property and that during a further *protection period* the seller will pay the commission to the broker if a sale occurs to any such person. The agreement may provide that this protection period obligation does not apply if the seller enters into a broker agreement with another broker and pays that broker in connection with a listing agreement.

A buyer who hires a broker can structure a commission agreement in a variety of ways. In essence the buyer agrees to pay the broker for finding a suitable property. With an *exclusive buyer's agreement*, the buyer will pay if the buyer purchases what the broker found. With such an agreement the buyer also may commit to notify the broker if the buyer becomes interested in a property not found by the broker. The typical agreement does not authorize the broker to make offers for the buyer without the buyer's agreement that the broker do so.

A broker can be entitled to a commission even without a written agreement.[26] The broker may be subject to disciplinary action by the N.C. Real Estate Commission for violating the regulations requiring broker agreements to be in writing, but this does not mean that the commission is necessarily forfeited if the existence of the essential elements of an agreement can be proved.[27] Under North Carolina law, the general rule is that a broker is entitled to be paid a commission by procuring a ready, willing, and able buyer to purchase at a price acceptable to the seller.[28] A broker is a *procuring cause* if the broker's efforts are the "direct and proximate" cause of the purchase. As the N.C. Supreme Court explained, the "term *procuring cause* refers to 'a cause originating or setting in motion a series of events which, without break in their continuity, result in the accomplishment of the prime object of the employment of the broker, which may variously be a sale or exchange of the principal's property, an ultimate agreement between the principal and a prospective contracting party, or the procurement of a purchaser who is ready, willing, and able to buy on the principal's terms.'"[29] This is most likely to be the case if the broker was the source of the seller's first contact with the buyer and the broker continues to be an intermediary.

A broker may be able to recover a commission even if the parties did not discuss a specific percentage or amount. A broker who is entitled to

---

26. Carver v. Britt, 241 N.C. 538, 540, 85 S.E.2d 888, 891 (1955).

27. 21 N.C.A.C. 58A .0104(a).

28. S & W Realty & Bonded Commercial Agency, Inc. v. Duckworth & Shelton, Inc., 274 N.C. 243, 250–51, 162 S.E.2d 486, 491 (1968).

29. *Id.* (quoting 12 Corpus Juris Secundum *Brokers* § 91 (1938) (emphasis in original)).

a commission by oral agreement as an authorized agent who enabled the events of a successful transaction would receive what the court or jury decides is a reasonable amount, which would be based on what is customary for the particular kind of property and brokerage services provided.

As between brokers, one broker's entitlement to share in a commission is a matter of the brokers' agreement. The client pays only what the client agreed to pay. For example, one broker could become entitled to a share of a commission from another broker by introducing the other broker to a buyer. It depends on what it is that the brokers agreed would earn a commission.[30]

3.3.5 Broker Liability for Fraud or Misrepresentation

Real estate buyers or sellers who believe they have been wronged by a broker sometimes use such terms as *fraud* to describe the situation. Proving fraud is difficult, however. Several facts must be proved for someone to prevail in such a claim. It must involve a misrepresentation of a fact that is *material* to the transaction, which means it must be important, that is, not inconsequential. The person who made the misrepresentation must have either known it was false or intentionally remained ignorant of it in a way intended to do harm. The person who made the representation also must have intended for the harmed person to rely on the misrepresentation.[31] In short, although fraud claims are often uttered, rarely are they successful in court.

A successful claim of fraud may result in a larger damage award than is possible with other kinds of claims based on false information. A related claim sometimes made against brokers as well as others is *negligent misrepresentation*. This occurs when someone provides false information on which someone relies without any reasonable basis for knowing it to be true; unlike fraud, the person providing the false information need not have actually known it was false. The person harmed by the misrepresentation must have acted reasonably in relying on it.[32]

A broker's potential liability for fraud or misrepresentation is greater than for someone who is just a party to a contract because a broker owes a client a fiduciary duty. This requires keeping clients informed of all facts

---

30. Maxwell v. Michael P. Doyle, Inc., 164 N.C. App. 319, 324–26, 595 S.E.2d 759, 762–63 (2004).

31. Powell v. Wold, 88 N.C. App. 61, 63–64, 362 S.E.2d 796, 797 (1987).

32. *Id.* at 67–68, 362 S.E.2d at 799.

material to the broker's representation. The courts have sustained a cause of action when brokers make false statements to their clients. For example, in one case a broker agreed with three others to handle the purchase and arrange financing. She allegedly reassured other investors that she had closed the deal and had obtained a deed to the real estate, when in fact the purchase had fallen through when unexpected obstacles had been encountered and a final agreement with the owners could not be reached. The court held that these misrepresentations were sufficient to sustain a jury's verdict of fraud and the award of punitive damages.[33]

Brokers commonly put their signs on real estate for which they have listings to identify it as being for sale and to give the broker's contact information. Similar information may be provided through a multiple listing service or on an Internet site. If the seller has entered into a contract and the broker continues to advertise the real estate as if it is for sale to others in the ordinary course, this could be a misleading attempt to conjure up business. Unfortunately some brokers may prefer not to update the advertisement so they can make contact with potential buyers and lead them to other available properties listed by the broker for other sellers. Or they may want to solicit buyers into hiring the broker as a buyer's broker. In any event, it causes buyers to make efforts based on a misimpression. Multiple listing services may require that brokers post information about contracts within a few days to alert buyers to the real status of the property's availability.

Claims of fraud or misrepresentation in a broker context more commonly arise when buyers believe they were tricked about the condition of the property. Typical circumstances that arise include serious flooding problems or impending changes in road access about which the seller knew but the buyer was unaware before the closing. The broker can become the subject of a lawsuit when the broker knew about the condition but did not disclose it in communications with the buyer. As the N.C. Supreme Court said, a "broker who makes fraudulent misrepresentations or who conceals a material fact when there is a duty to speak to a prospective purchaser in connection with the sale of the principal's property is personally liable to the purchaser notwithstanding that the broker was acting in the capacity of agent for the seller."[34] This means that brokers cannot use their duty to

---

33. Carter v. Parsons, 61 N.C. App. 412, 301 S.E.2d 405 (1983).

34. Johnson v. Beverly-Hanks & Assocs., Inc., 328 N.C. 202, 210, 400 S.E.2d 38, 43 (1991) (emphasis omitted) (quoting P. HETRICK & J. MCLAUGHLIN, WEBSTER'S REAL

protect their clients' interests as sellers to mislead buyers into thinking a known problem does not exist. As the court also said, a "broker has a duty not to conceal from the purchasers any material facts and to make full and open disclosure of all such information."[35]

The broker's disclosure obligation applies to *material* facts *known* to the broker. The cases in which brokers have been held liable for misrepresentation, fraud, or unfair trade practices involve clear instances in which the broker had specific information that obviously would have been important to the buyer's decision. Brokers do not have an obligation to investigate property conditions for the parties, however. For example, in one case the N.C. Court of Appeals rejected a claim by buyers against a seller's broker alleging that the broker breached a duty to the buyers by not checking flood maps to determine whether the property was vulnerable to flooding. The broker did not make any representations about flooding, and the court said the buyers had full opportunity to investigate the matter themselves and the broker was not responsible for doing it for them.[36] In other words, brokers are not responsible for alerting buyers to something that would have become known if only they had paid attention to information about which a reasonable person would be expected to inquire.

The courts interpret the law as expecting buyers to make their own reasonable investigations. Those who fail to do so may not be able to hold a broker liable for an incorrect statement about the property condition. For instance, the N.C. Court of Appeals held that buyers who were foiled in their plans to open a restaurant because the septic system proved inadequate could not hold the seller's broker liable for allegedly saying that the system would be adequate for such a purpose. The court focused on the fact that the broker did not induce the buyers into foregoing an inspection of the system. The court explained that "claims based upon misrepresentations are groundless where a purchaser of real property 'deals at arm[']s length and the purchaser has full opportunity to make inquiry but neglects to do so and the seller resorted to no artifice which was reasonably calculated to induce the purchaser to forego investigation.'"[37]

Estate Law in North Carolina § 132, at 165 (3d ed. 1988)).

35. *Id.*

36. Clouse v. Gordon, 115 N.C. App. 500, 445 S.E.2d 428 (1994).

37. Hearne v. Statesville Lodge No. 687, 143 N.C. App. 560, 561, 546 S.E.2d 414, 415 (2001) (quoting Calloway v. Wyatt, 246 N.C. 129, 134, 97 S.E.2d 881, 885–86 (1957)).

Brokers are often asked to give their general opinion about such things as the desirability of a neighborhood, the quality of schools, or the likelihood of new development. These kinds of generalized opinions are not the kind of factual misrepresentations that can properly form the basis for liability.[38] But courts have sustained claims against brokers who had specific information and clearly misled others when asked. For example, the N.C. Court of Appeals allowed claims of fraud and misrepresentation to proceed based on a broker's failure to mention that she knew a major road extension was planned close to the subject property when the buyers who hired her asked if there was any factor known to the broker that would adversely affect the value of the property.[39] In another case, the court held that a claim could be sustained when a broker failed to share information as soon as possible that showed that a lot was smaller than had been represented to the buyers when they signed an offer to purchase. The broker had waited until the closing to correct the misimpression.[40]

A person who is harmed by a broker's egregious action can make a claim for triple damages plus payment of lawyers' fees under North Carolina's Unfair and Deceptive Trade Practices Act, which is intended to protect consumers.[41] An award for triple damages and lawyers' fees award is not automatic. Someone seeking this kind of remedy must prove that the broker's practice was unfair or deceptive.[42] Even an obvious violation of the Real Estate Commission's regulations is not by itself a basis for an enhanced award under this statute. It is available based on fraud.[43]

3.3.6 Broker Escrows

In a typical home sale, the broker holds the buyer's money on deposit as an escrow agent. North Carolina brokers must deposit funds in a trust or escrow account with a North Carolina bank or savings and loan within three banking days and may not comingle the money with the broker's own funds. Nothing requires brokers to put the money in interest-bearing accounts. They can do so but first must receive the parties' written authorization, and the authorization must specify how and to whom the interest

---

38. Carpenter v. Merrill Lynch Realty Operating P'ship, L.P., 108 N.C. App. 555, 560, 424 S.E.2d 178, 180 (1993).
39. Powell v. Wold, 88 N.C. App. 61, 362 S.E.2d 796 (1987).
40. Edwards v. West, 128 N.C. App. 570, 495 S.E.2d 920 (1998).
41. *Powell*, 88 N.C. App. at 68, 362 S.E.2d at 800.
42. G.S. 75-1.1; G.S. 75-16; G.S. 75-16.1.
43. *Powell*, 88 N.C. App. at 69, 362 S.E.2d at 800.

will be paid.[44] Brokers must maintain complete records of the money they receive, and the Real Estate Commission may inspect these records.

The broker escrow arrangement has a natural potential for conflicting tendencies. The broker is most likely to be paid a commission from what is to be paid to the seller and therefore has a financial incentive to cause the closing to occur. At the same time, the broker is holding a substantial sum deposited by the buyer. If the buyer learns something unfavorable about the property, or has difficulty obtaining financing, the buyer may prefer to withdraw the deposit and purchase another property.

The potential for conflict can be minimized with clear instructions that do not give the escrow agent discretion that could be exercised to the advantage of either party. A broker functioning as escrow agent is bound to comply with the escrow instructions and deliver the deposit only upon satisfaction of the instructions' conditions. An escrow holder can be held liable for breach of fiduciary duty or negligence for violating the instructions or exceeding the granted authority.

Buyers who enter into a real estate contract and make an escrow deposit with a broker should not be under the impression that a deposit with a broker can easily be withdrawn. Nor should sellers expect that a broker will release the deposit if the seller believes that the buyer has reneged. Sometimes the parties agree to cancel the contract and jointly give the broker written instructions to release the deposit or to split it in a way agreed upon by the parties. But the parties often do not agree, and the broker cannot act as judge and decide who should get the deposit. Parties should understand that the escrow can be tied up and that there can be the need for court action, which has an additional cost to those involved.

If there is a dispute over rights to the escrow the broker must hold it until the parties resolve their dispute by agreement or there is a court order that resolves it. A special proceeding in the superior courts is available for resolving the dispute. The broker must first give the parties ninety days' prior notice by mail of intent to start the superior court action. If the escrow being held by the broker is deposited with the court, the superior court clerk will determine proper ownership of it.[45]

---

44. 21 N.C.A.C. 58A .0107(b).
45. G.S. 93A-12.

3.4 Lawyers

Nothing in the law requires a seller or buyer to hire a lawyer to handle a real estate transaction. Lawyers commonly do represent parties in real estate transactions and for good reasons. For a buyer, a lawyer can investigate title and explain identifiable risks, arrange for title insurance, and ensure that the necessary instruments are properly prepared and recorded. For a seller, a lawyer can prepare the deed and other closing documents in a way that meets the contract requirements, check for proper purchase price allocations, and ensure that the necessary instruments are recorded to protect the seller's interests. For all concerned, lawyers can advise their clients about the seriousness of complications and provide advice about how to handle them.

Most real estate transactions are unexceptional and completed in what seems to be a routine manner. This does not mean, though, that any transaction should be taken lightly. Many aspects of real estate transactions entail legal hazards, and someone who is not a lawyer may not understand these risks, know when there are reasons for concern, or understand how to address complications when they arise. A lawyer's knowledge and experience can help individuals avoid problems and minimize their impact.

Parties to real estate transactions can decide to handle matters for themselves rather than hire lawyers. But a person who is not licensed to practice law in North Carolina may not perform functions or services that constitute the practice of law for someone else. A nonlawyer who is not working under the direct supervision of an active member of the state bar would be engaged in unauthorized practice of law if he or she performs any of the following functions for another: prepares a deed or deed of trust, provides an opinion about title, or provides an opinion about legal rights or obligations.[46] Only lawyers may explain or recommend a course of action to a party to a transaction under circumstances that require the exercise of legal judgment or that have implications with respect to the party's legal rights or obligations.

Nonlawyers may assist lawyers in these functions under their direct supervision. A nonlawyer may handle administrative duties in connection with a closing. Often such duties are handled by a paralegal who works with a law firm or title company.[47] Assistants may present and identify the

---

46. G.S. 84-2.1; G.S. 84-4.

47. N.C. State Bar, Authorized Practice Advisory Opinion 2002-1: On the Role of Laypersons in the Consummation of Residential Real Estate Transactions (Jan. 24, 2003), *available at* www.ncbar.gov/programs/auth_notes.asp; N.C. State Bar, 2002 Formal

documents at closing, ensure that the documents are properly signed, and handle the closing payments. They work under lawyers' supervision and must refer questions that involve legal advice to the lawyers.

3.4.1 Choosing a Lawyer

A special license is not required for a lawyer to handle a real estate matter, but within the legal community real estate transactions generally are considered to be a field for which some experience, or affiliation with an experienced real estate lawyer, is appropriate before representation is undertaken. Many lawyers have such experience. Generalists tend to include real estate transactions within their practices, and for ordinary transactions there are many choices for competent representation. A good way to find a competent lawyer to handle a common legal matter is by referral from someone else who has had a positive experience with a lawyer handling a similar matter. Brokers and bankers may have recommendations. Although in many cases this is based on positive experiences and is helpful, it also may be based on inappropriate favoritism. Before agreeing to representation, the client should therefore ask enough questions to be comfortable about the lawyers' experience and apparent readiness to provide competent and timely service.

3.4.2 Fees

There is no standard lawyer's fee for preparing a deed, doing title work, or handling a closing, but fees for such services tend to be comparable within a community. Lawyers should be able to provide a fairly reliable estimate of what these routine services will cost. Lawyers often charge a flat fee for such services that is likely to be comparable with fees that other lawyers in the same community charge for the same services. For representation that requires more than preparation of a fairly standard document, most lawyers charge on an hourly basis for their time and for the time of legal assistants to whom they delegate work on the matter.

For most kinds of legal representation there is no requirement that a fee agreement be put in writing. Even though it is not required, many lawyers provide an *engagement letter* that outlines the scope of the representation and any specific client goals, especially for new client–lawyer relationships.

Ethics Opinion 9: Delegation to Nonlawyer Assistant of Certain Tasks Associated with a Residential Real Estate Transaction (Jan. 24, 2003), *available at* www.ncbar.com/ethics/ethics.asp?id=655.

Engagement letters typically provide information about the responsible lawyer's fee structure and billing procedures, the identity of other lawyers and specialists who may work on the file and their rates, and any requirements for client approval before other individuals work on the file. Some clients, including government units subject to public finance constraints, also require an initial and periodically updated budget of anticipated fees and expenses, and specify a billing format and schedule for their lawyers to use.

3.4.3 Confidentiality and Conflicts of Interest

The *attorney–client privilege* enables clients to communicate with their lawyers confidentially. The privilege is intended to allow clients to be candid with their lawyers to obtain the best possible advice. Confidentiality also allows lawyers to share frank advice with their clients. The privilege of confidentiality belongs to the client. Only the client has the power to agree to disclose information that is otherwise confidential. There are a few narrow exceptions to this obligation, including a lawyer's professional duty to comply with a law or court order and to disclose information reasonably believed necessary to prevent fraud.

According to the standard rules of professional conduct, a lawyer may not represent multiple clients if there is significant risk that responsibilities to a client will be materially limited by other loyalties, unless the lawyer reasonably believes that competent and diligent representation can be provided to each client. When such potential exists and the lawyer does reasonably believe such representation can be provided, the lawyer must inform each client of the situation and get written consent.

Residential real estate transactions are unusual in the way lawyers often may represent more than one party in the same transaction, such as both the buyer and seller, or the buyer and the buyer's lender. This is permissible in many circumstances because the lawyer's role is considered to be confined to matters for which there is no real conflict. In the usual real estate transaction, the lawyer gets involved based on a contract that already exists. If the buyer's and seller's interests are generally aligned and the lawyer determines that the potential for a conflict can be managed, the lawyer can represent both. The same is true for representing a buyer and the buyer's mortgage lender. For example, in most cases a lawyer may represent both the borrower and the lender, prepare the deed, and draft other documents as may be necessary to complete the transaction.[48] When representing multiple clients the lawyer is required to advise them all of the risks of common representation and their right to separate counsel. If circumstances change and the interests diverge, the lawyer must withdraw from representing everyone in the transaction.[49]

These presumptions about dual representation apply to typical residential closings. In a commercial real estate transaction, the parties' interests are not as likely to be so closely aligned that one lawyer may properly represent both the buyer and the seller. The parties usually use their own lawyers to negotiate the contract, and even after the contract has been agreed upon there are likely to be differing interests in interpreting whether or not conditions in the contract have been satisfied, and other matters may arise about which a lawyer's judgment will be very specific to one but not both sides of the transaction.

Although the rules that govern lawyers' conduct may permit common representation, the parties involved should consider whether this is their preference. For example, if a seller has not disclosed a title problem or serious structural flaw and is considering whether further disclosure is required or appropriate, a lawyer who also represents the buyer may not be able to give objective advice about disclosure. Similarly, if one party is considering terminating the agreement because it appears the other has breached it, the lawyer may not be able to represent both parties objectively. In this kind of situation seeking an independent lawyer's advice probably is appropriate.

Those who engage lawyers should also consider how to define their relationship with respect to the lawyers' communications with others. Everyone is familiar with a lawyer's ability to make decisions for the client in specific circumstances, such as at trial. Lawyers often speak for their clients in other contexts, such as negotiations, but they do not have unfettered authority to do so. According to the lawyers' rules of professional conduct, lawyers have discretion to make decisions about the means for pursuing

---

48. N.C. State Bar, Ethics Opinion RPC 210: Representation of Multiple Parties to the Closing of a Residential Real Estate Transaction (Apr. 4, 1997), *available at* www.ncbar.com/ethics/ethics.asp?id=210; N.C. State Bar, 97 Formal Ethics Opinion 8: Representation of Developer and Buyer in Closing of a Residential Real Estate Transaction (Jan. 16, 1998), *available at* www.ncbar.com/ethics/ethics.asp?page=6&from=1/1998.

49. N.C. State Bar, Rule of Professional Conduct 1.7: Conflict of Interest: Current Clients, *available at* www.ncbar.com/rules/rpcsearch.asp; N.C. State Bar, Ethics Opinion CPR 100 (Apr. 15, 1977), *available at* www.ncbar.com/ethics/index.asp.

their clients' objectives, such as what motions to file and what witnesses to call in a case, but lawyers must consult with their clients about significant decisions and keep them informed about details.[50] Ultimately the client and lawyer can always agree on the extent of the lawyer's actual authority.

3.5 Deeds

Most transfers of real estate from one person to another are accomplished with a deed. Despite the familiar nature of what looks to be a deed, each deed is unique, and the implication of its details can involve an understanding of many different legal principles. No one should presume to be able to prepare a deed based solely on the kind of general information provided in this book. Yet some knowledge of the basics can be helpful for understanding the significance of a deed and the rights and risks it entails.

3.5.1 Deed Contents

Deeds tend to be in a customary format. They commonly contain the following elements, in this order: name and address of the person giving the deed, known as the *grantor*; a statement that payment has been made, known as *consideration*; words expressing an intent to grant or give the deed, such as "does hereby convey"; the name and address of the person receiving, known as the *grantee*; a statement of warranties given by the grantor (see Sections 3.5.1.1–3); a description of the land involved and what may be specifically excluded; and the grantor's notarized signature. Many deeds also contain reference information about the chain of title, such as the recording information for the deed by which the grantor acquired title, or provide other information about what is intended to be conveyed, such as a reference to a plan. Such references give further information about the grantor's intent and links to evidence for confirming the grantor's title.

The usual arrangement of information on a deed that has been recorded is depicted in Figure 1.

As noted in that form, the person giving the deed is referred to as *grantor*; the person receiving it, as *grantee*. Although most deeds adhere to what is customary, the parties to the transfer decide how they are going to

---

50. N.C. State Bar, Rule of Professional Conduct 1.2: Scope of Representation and Allocation of Authority between Client and Lawyer, and Rule of Professional Conduct 1.4: Communication, both *available at* www.ncbar.com/rules/rpcsearch.asp.

Figure 1. Arrangement of information on a recorded deed

Bk: ___ pg: ___

The book and page of the records
at which this instrument can be found

Recording Fee: _____
Excise tax: _____

The recording fees and excise tax paid

Brief description for the index: _____

A short description that will be used in the index to identify the property

Date: ___

Date deed is given

GRANTOR: _____   **GRANTEE:** _____

Name of the grantor (seller)   *Name of the grantee (buyer)*

_____ **DEED**

The type of warranties being given: general warranty, quitclaim, etc.

Grantor for valuable consideration paid by Grantee . . . conveys . . . the lot or parcel of land situated in _____ **more particularly described as follows:**

Property description

Reference to a recorded plan that shows the property

Reference to deed by which the grantor acquired the property

Any exceptions from the property acquired by the grantor,
not being conveyed to the grantee of this deed

Name of grantor

_____

Signature of grantor

Notary acknowledgment of grantor's signature;
notary's seal, signature, and commission expiration date

describe what it is that is being transferred. This includes not only the kind of warranties being given but also how the real estate is to be described. In most cases a grantor wants to describe just what is already owned, so most deeds repeat descriptions from prior deeds. As described in Section 2.2, a variety of methods are used for describing the real estate. The most common includes a reference to a recorded plan or a metes and bounds real estate description. Whatever method of description is used, it will be sufficient if the intent of the person giving the deed can be determined. Minor discrepancies or typographical errors usually can be seen for just what they are and do not cause a problem. But if something is omitted, or the description is so problematic that the intent cannot be determined, disputes can arise between the person who gave the deed and the person who received it or between adjoining landowners both of whom claim the same land. In this case, if those who are having the dispute cannot reach an agreement, a trial may be necessary, and the court will consider available evidence to try to determine what was intended.

Deeds usually only describe land boundaries. People naturally include buildings when they think of real estate. But the deeds on which they rely usually describe only the land and refer to "improvements thereon" in a general sense, with no specific mention of buildings. This is partly a result of custom but also because land boundary descriptions can remain the same forever and buildings and other improvements change over time, including during the interval between acquiring real estate by deed and conveying it away by another deed.

There is no requirement that the contents of a deed state how much is being paid for the real estate. In North Carolina, the price can be seen on the public record based on the stamp showing how much excise tax was paid, which, as described in Section 1.5.2, is a percentage of what was paid for the real estate as reported by the person recording the deed. If the deed is not subject to the tax, such as is the case for a transfer by a government unit, nothing on the deed will show how much was paid. Traditionally, lawyers were concerned that the absence of information in the body of the deed about how much is being paid could be an opportunity for a claim that the deed was invalid because nothing was paid. To address this issue, deeds usually contain a statement that consideration has been paid for the conveyance with such words as "for consideration paid" without saying how much. In modern times this seems to add little because the question still remains what was actually paid if there is a question about the transfer's validity. Even more confusing, drafters sometimes say for "a dollar and other consideration" or "ten dollars and other consideration" as a gesture of the deed signor's acknowledgment that a payment was made. This kind of gesture is an odd remnant of a custom.

In addition to this kind of common information, deeds may contain any other information that is necessary to describe what is being conveyed or to make clear what is not being conveyed. Much of a deed can be understood by someone without legal training, but care must be exercised because terms used in deeds may have significance beyond their plain meaning. In that case an experienced real estate lawyer's advice may be necessary to understand what is being conveyed.

A deed is often referred to by the nature of the warranty being given by the grantor to the grantee. A deed with general warranties is therefore referred to as a *warranty deed*. A discussion of the basic nature of these forms follows.

3.5.1.1 Warranty or General Warranty

The most common form of deed is a *warranty deed*. The grantor promises lawful possession free of others' rights except as disclosed in the deed; that no one else's participation is needed for the rights to be conveyed; that there are no mortgages or other liens except as stated in the deed; and that the grantor will defend the title against claims that breach these warranties.

3.5.1.2 Special Warranty

With a special warranty deed, the grantor gives only limited assurances to the grantee. A grantor giving special warranty covenants gives a warranty against any prior transfers *by the grantor*, including prior conveyances of the premises, mortgages, and the creation of easements or other rights in the land if they arose by or through the grantor. In most instances, a quitclaim deed is given because the grantor is unsure about title and does not want the liabilities that accompany a warranty deed. In some states this type of deed is called a quitclaim deed, which in North Carolina is different, as described below.

3.5.1.3 Quitclaim

In North Carolina, a conveyance by quitclaim deed is a conveyance *as is*. It is normally used in circumstances in which the title is unclear or in dispute. By taking real estate with a quitclaim deed, the grantee assumes the burden of having to overcome this uncertain state when seeking mortgage financing or later trying to convey the real estate. A quitclaim deed is commonly used when two parties both claim a portion of real estate and with a settlement one conveys all rights to the other.

3.5.2 Signatories

A deed can convey only what the grantor received by deed or other means. In most cases the grantor's name will match exactly the name on an earlier-recorded deed by which the grantor acquired title. Minor differences, such as initials, may be easily explained, and changes that are explained in the deed—such as use of a new, married name and reference to the name by which the spouse was previously known—will not cause a problem. But variations that leave some reasonable doubt about the identity of the grantor could create a cloud that must be addressed with investigation and additional documentation. This could include variations that may be common in other contexts, such as the use of a nickname. Drafters and title searchers therefore take great care with the form of a name on a real estate instrument.

Sometimes real estate is conveyed by a legal representative, such as by someone with a power of attorney. Someone who gives a power to someone to sign legal instruments is known as a *principal*, and the person who receives the power is known as an *attorney-in-fact*. The scope of the power depends on the instrument giving it; a *general power of attorney* gives the attorney-in-fact the power to act in all legal matters, and a *special power of attorney* restricts that power to a specific transaction or transactions, such as signing a deed, deed of trust, and other instruments for conveyances of specific real estate. When a real estate instrument is recorded that has been signed by an attorney-in-fact, the power of attorney is recorded along with the instrument to show that the proper authority existed. There are many other types of representatives who may have the authority to sign for another, such as a trustee or commissioner. In each case evidence of the proper authority should be apparent.

Entities and government units also act through their representatives. Real estate instruments conveying their interests will be signed by an individual who indicates such a capacity, such as a manager for a limited liability company or a county manager for a county. Whether a particular individual actually has authority to sign a deed or other instrument depends on that particular individual's capacity and the nature of the property being transferred. For example, by statute a board of directors has the authority to convey a corporation's real estate in the ordinary course of business, and that authority may be delegated to an officer of the corporation.[51] If the conveyance is not in the ordinary course of business, such as a conveyance of all of the property of a corporation that is not in the business of owning and conveying property, a vote of the shareholders may be required.[52] Although the basic nature of authority to sign an instrument and bind an entity is set by statute, the entity can set its own rules in its governing documents. Accordingly, lawyers commonly will require further documentation of specific authority, such as a copy of a corporation's current bylaws and a resolution by the shareholders and directors confirming an officer's actual authority to sign a deed. As another example, by statute limited liability company managers have the authority to convey real estate for their companies, but lawyers commonly require a resolution by the company's members about a manager's actual authority.

Deeds and other instruments for conveyances by government entities also are signed by representatives, and the specifics of who are proper signatories also depend on statutes and governing charters. For example, county commissioners have ultimate authority to approve county conveyances, but in their governing documents or by specific resolution they may authorize the county manager to sign deeds.[53] State agency authority also may be specified by statute or resolution.

There are restrictions on when government units may convey property. For example, local governments are required to sell real estate by public auction unless it is being exchanged for other property or is being conveyed to certain kinds of organizations or individuals for specific purposes.[54] Conveyances of particular kinds of property also can be restricted by statute, such as real estate subject to a public right-of-way, or it can be restricted by deed, such as real estate acquired with a covenant that it be used only for a certain purpose. Each conveyance by a government unit therefore potentially involves special considerations.

3.5.3 Recordability

To be recordable with the register of deeds a deed must conform to legal requirements in a number of respects. A deed or deed of trust executed after January 1, 1980, must show, on the first page, the name of the law firm

---

51. G.S. 55-8-41; G.S. 55-12-01.
52. G.S. 55-12-02.
53. G.S. 153A-82.
54. G.S. 153A-176; G.S. 160A-265; G.S. 160A-266.

or person who drafted the instrument.[55] County commissioners also may adopt a resolution that imposes additional requirements in their counties. They may require that instruments have the grantee's or the owner's permanent mailing address.[56] If a county uses parcel identifier numbers (PINs), it may require these numbers to be shown on the instrument and verified by the county before a deed can be recorded.[57] The county commissioners may require the register of deeds to refuse to record a deed unless it has the tax assessor's notation that the instrument has been presented to the assessor and the necessary information has been obtained from it.[58] Some counties use this procedure; others elect to follow a set of procedures that require the register to furnish information to the tax assessor after the instrument is recorded.[59] The statutes authorize the commissioners in most of the counties to prohibit recording of a deed unless the county tax collector certifies on it that there are no delinquent taxes that constitute a lien on the subject real estate.[60] If the commissioners adopt such a requirement, a register must nonetheless accept a deed for registration without the tax collector's certification if the deed contains the following statement: "This instrument prepared by: _____, a licensed North Carolina attorney. Delinquent taxes, if any, to be paid by the closing attorney to the county tax collector upon disbursement of closing proceeds."[61] Several counties have been separately authorized by state laws to require all delinquent real estate taxes be paid on a parcel of land before a deed to that parcel may be recorded.

Presenters should check with any county to which a deed will be presented for current recording requirements and fees.

3.6 Closings

The event at which real estate is transferred from the seller to the buyer is called a *closing*. A closing usually involves at least three parties: seller, buyer, and lender. Others who may attend are those who are managing the

---

55. G.S. 47-17.1.
56. G.S. 161-30(a).
57. G.S. 161-30(b).
58. G.S. 105-303(a)(2).
59. G.S. 105-303(a)(1).
60. G.S. 161-31.
61. G.S. 161-31(a1), (b).

closing or who have a financial interest in it, such as a lawyer handling the transaction for the buyer or a broker expecting a commission.

At a typical closing, the two key instruments signed before a notary and immediately recorded with the register of deeds are the deed and deed of trust. Many other documents will be prepared and signed at the closing or before, including a settlement statement showing all charges and disbursements, and other forms used to comply with regulations. Commercial closings are likely to involve many other matters and documents.

Years ago closings occurred at the register of deeds office, but today it is more likely to be at a lawyer's or title company's office. A lawyer or someone under a lawyer's supervision will handle the document completion and disbursements and delivery of documents to the register of deeds office. Although the steps are usually straightforward, the process is complicated because it involves several simultaneous and interrelated events. For instance, the real estate being sold usually is subject to an existing loan owed by the seller that is the subject of a deed of trust tying up the real estate. The buyer and the buyer's lender want the real estate free of this deed of trust, but the seller needs money from the buyer's loan to pay off the seller's loan. The closing therefore essentially involves simultaneous exchanges of funds and interests, and each step of the process depends on completion of another step. To resolve the circular problem involving loans, a new lender is usually willing to disburse a loan for a purchase as long as that lender is assured that the funds are being applied to pay off all existing security interests because the new lender knows that the prior lender must eventually provide the satisfaction instrument and leave the new lender with the only effective security instrument on record.

Those who handle a closing must ensure that these events proceed as planned and that the registration of the deed, deed of trust, and satisfaction instrument occur in proper sequence without anything intervening on the record that might affect the rights of the parties involved. Consequently, any delay in recording, such as might occur if new information appears on the record or if there is a problem getting an instrument accepted for registration, may be perceived as a substantial risk by those responsible for the closing.

3.6.1 Settlement Statement

For any closing involving a federally related loan, which includes most residential transactions, a form known as the HUD-1 settlement statement will be completed. HUD refers to the U.S. Department of Housing and Urban

Development. The form, also commonly used by banks and lawyers even when not required, is intended to provide understandable and complete disclosure of all costs in connection with a closing. But someone who has not worked with the form can find it to be very confusing.

HUD-1 form has two pages (usually but not always on both sides of one sheet of paper). Items being charged to the buyer and seller for the closing are listed on one side. The other shows the accounting of these items against the purchase price and adjustments to the purchase price for such things as release of the deposit and real estate tax adjustments based on the date of closing. One column of the accounting shows the calculation from the buyer's perspective; the other column the calculation from the seller's perspective.

By federal law all charges in connection with the closing must be shown separately, whether deducted or added to the purchase price or paid *outside the closing* by one of the parties. For a buyer and seller the most important aspect of the settlement statement is the opportunity to examine every charge and confirm it is consistent with what was understood. If not, the lawyer or other professional handling the closing should be able to explain.

3.6.2 Tax Reporting

An excise tax must be paid in relation to most real estate transfers in North Carolina (see Section 1.5.2). The usual residential transaction does not involve federal or state income taxes or sales tax. Commercial transactions do have tax implications. Regardless of whether a state or federal tax must be paid, most transactions must be reported to the Internal Revenue Service (IRS).

In general, the seller of real estate realizes a taxable gain for federal tax purposes to the extent that cash received exceeds the seller's *adjusted basis* for the real estate, which in general is the amount the seller paid for the real estate plus certain expenditures. The federal tax code provides a *home-sale gain exclusion rule* that excludes from taxation gains from the sale of a principal residence. The rule is subject to certain limits, including on the amount excluded and the time during which the residence must have been owned and used.[62] In most cases the result is no tax owed on the sale of a residence. A lawyer or accountant should be consulted to determine

---

62. Internal Revenue Service, *Selling Your Home*, Pub. 523 (for 2011 returns), *available at* www.irs.gov/pub/irs-pdf/p523.pdf.

whether a sale is subject to federal or state taxes and what returns must be filed.

Several tax credits or deductions have recently been allowed as special incentives to home buyers. These may enable a buyer to deduct a portion of the purchase price against other income, for a substantial tax advantage. Credits or deductions may be available for home improvements or energy enhancements. Current law should be checked, and a tax professional consulted, when the current tax rules are unclear.

Regardless of whether a tax is owed, the person handling a real estate conveyance transaction may have a federal tax reporting obligation. Under Section 6045 of the Internal Revenue Code, one of the following persons, in order, must file, with the IRS, Form 1099, which includes the parties' Social Security or taxpayer identification numbers and information about the transaction: the person (including any lawyer or title company) responsible for closing the transaction; the mortgage lender; the seller's broker; the buyer's broker; or such other person designated in regulations prescribed by the treasury secretary. Certain transactions are not subject to the reporting requirements, but most persons handling closings file a Form 1099 in all cases rather than risk making determinations about the applicability of the exceptions in a particular case.

3.7 Recording

A deed does not have to be recorded for real estate ownership to be transferred from the seller to the buyer. But the buyer takes a great risk if the deed is not recorded. Without recording the deed, no one could be certain about who the current legal owner is, and a buyer would be always vulnerable to having someone else claim to already have a deed for the same real estate. The real estate recording system is intended to provide a mechanism for a buyer to confirm the rights of someone offering to convey and for those who legitimately acquire real estate interests to protect themselves against wrongful claims. In North Carolina all one hundred counties have an elected register of deeds who manages a public office for such recording.

3.7.1 Recording and Priorities

Although the notion of recording seems straightforward, there are complicated legal rules that come into play when there is a question about who has a better right to real estate among competing claimants. Each state has its own set of recording laws. North Carolina is one of the few states with a *pure race* recording statute. This statute provides that no deed or other instrument of conveyance "shall be valid to pass any property interest as against lien creditors or purchasers for a valuable consideration from the donor, bargainor or lessor but from the time of registration thereof in the county where the land lies."[63] This is called the pure race rule because only registration of the instrument matters when determining which of two recorded deeds for the same real estate is enforceable. This means that unless a court applies a narrow exception based on fraud or another rarely applied theory, those who record first will have title. This also means it is very important to record instruments immediately.

3.7.2 Recording Requirements

Registers of deeds do not review instruments presented to them to determine if they are legally valid. They do not check or confirm that an instrument creates ownership rights. Registers only review presented instruments to see if they meet the format and minimum content requirements.

One recording requirement that registers enforce is the presence of a notary acknowledgment or other authorized official's acknowledgment of the party's signature, and this applies to deeds and deeds of trust. This requirement also applies to a number of other common instruments, including a contract for real estate, a lease, a marriage settlement, a satisfaction instrument, and power of attorney.[64] When in doubt drafters should consult the current version of the statutes to see whether particular kinds of instruments require notarizations.

The usual form of notarization is an acknowledgment through which a notary or other authorized official states that he or she saw the person sign the document. The basic form of acknowledgment certificate is shown in Figure 2.

An alternative is a *proof,* which is when a person certifies under oath or affirmation to a notary or other authorized official that the person witnessed someone else execute, record, or acknowledge a record. The basic form of proof certificate for an individual is shown in Figure 3.

---

63. G.S. 47-18(a) (deeds, contracts); G.S. 47-20 (deeds of trust and other security instruments); G.S. 47-27 (easements).
64. G.S. 47-17; G.S. 47-25.

Figure 2. Acknowledgment certificate

_____ County, North Carolina

I certify that the following person(s) personally appeared before me this day, each acknowledging to me that he or she voluntarily signed the foregoing document for the purpose stated therein and in the capacity indicated: _name(s) of principals_.

Date: _____

(Official Seal)   _official signature of notary_
                       notary's typed name, Notary Public
                       My commission expires: _____

Figure 3. Proof certificate

_____ County, North Carolina

I certify that _name of subscribing witness_ personally appeared before me this day and certified to me under oath or by affirmation that he or she is not a named party to the foregoing document, has no interest in the transaction, signed the foregoing document as a subscribing witness, and either (i) witnessed _name of principal_ (the principal) sign the foregoing document or (ii) witnessed the principal acknowledge the principal's signature on the already signed document.

Date: _____

(Official Seal)   _official signature of notary_
                       notary's typed name, Notary Public
                       My commission expires: _____

Some documents instead require an oath or affirmation, which is when an individual makes a vow of truthfulness before the official and a _jurat_ is completed. An example of such a document is an _affidavit_, which records someone's statement under oath. With an oath, the individual whose action is being observed invokes a deity or uses any form of the word _swear_; with an affirmation the person makes a vow based on personal honor without invoking a deity or using the word _swear_. The basic form for jurat certificate for an individual is shown in Figure 4.

If, after reviewing the proof or acknowledgment of execution the register of deeds decides that a signature cannot be verified and therefore that the instrument cannot be registered, the individual seeking to record

Figure 4. Jurat certificate

_____ County, North Carolina

Signed and sworn to (or affirmed) before me this day by _name of principal_.

Date: _____

(Official Seal)   _official signature of notary_
                         notary's typed name, Notary Public
                         My commission expires: _____

the instrument may apply to the district court of the county for an order directing the register to record the instrument.[65] To issue the order, however, the district court must find that the instrument meets the verification requirements.[66]

Under North Carolina law, in addition to notaries, specified other officials may perform acknowledgments, and before registering the document the register will check the North Carolina statute to see that a person with the designated capacity is among those who are authorized.[67] Within North Carolina, the authorized officials include notaries, judges and clerks of court, federal consular officials and military officers, and North Carolina magistrates. Note that the register considers whether the officer has _apparent_ authority for registration purposes. The register does not check to determine whether the person actually has the authority indicated. Nor does the register investigate whether the law of another state would authorize the official to take an acknowledgment. For the purpose of recording a document, the register relies on the list of authorized officials in the North Carolina statute. The register will check for the certificate and for the official's signature, a seal (if one is required, as for a notary), and the official's expiration date.

In addition to notarization, as discussed in Section 3.5.3, sometimes certain other information must be included on particular instruments, such as the name of the drafter on a deed or a deed of trust. Registers also check for certain statewide format requirements, such as a size of either 8½ by 11 or 8½ by 14, certain minimum margins and font size, use of only

---

65. G.S. 47-14(b).
66. _Id._
67. G.S. 47-1; G.S. 47-2.

one side, and the presence of a title. Noncompliance with a number of format requirements incurs an additional fee.[68] Presenters should check with registers for current requirements.

3.7.3 Title Searches

A deed is recorded to give what is known as *constructive notice* to anyone who might later be interested in the real estate. Everyone can see recorded instruments by checking the register's records, and the law considers everyone to be aware of the document regardless of whether it has actually been seen. Consequently, to determine rights to real estate based on the recorded instruments, the searcher looks for a *chain of title* of conveyances from one owner to another. The links in this chain are found by looking for the names of the various owners who have passed along the real estate. In the register of deeds system, any person named in an instrument as receiving an interest in real estate is known as a *grantee*, and any person who gave it is known as a *grantor*. So with a deed the seller is a grantor and the buyer is a grantee, and with a deed of trust the owner is a grantor and the lender and trustee are grantees. In most cases involving a typical real estate instrument such as these, the identity of the parties is obvious, but in some cases the register must interpret the legal intent of an instrument for which the drafter has not clearly identified the parties. It is possible for one person to be both a grantor and grantee, as when two adjoining owners agree to share some aspect of their properties, thereby making each a grantee and a grantor. In North Carolina, documents are recorded strictly in the order in which they are presented to the register of deeds and can be found with an index of the names of the parties to the instruments.

Current claims in real estate can only be determined by examining the publicly recorded documents in the chain of title for that real estate as well as other available information about the real estate in other records. Those who purchase real estate, or give loans in exchange for a deed of trust, must rely on professionals to perform this research and analysis. The records' reliability depends on the public's ability to find what affects particular real estate. Although there are many standard approaches to drafting real estate instruments, the parties are free to draft them according to their intent, and wide variations exist. A register of deeds office may have millions of documents on file. The indexing system is therefore

---

68. G.S. 161-10(a)(18a); G.S. 161-14(b).

essential for finding documents that apply to the real estate of interest. The register keeps an index with the names of the parties to the instrument. Registers of deeds follow standards for indexing adopted by the registers' association and lawyers' bar and approved by the N.C. Secretary of State.[69] Registers may also adopt internal rules and are required to post them in their offices.[70]

The indexes are divided into human and nonhuman name sections, and in each section the names are entered strictly in alphabetical order. Human names are sorted first by surname and then by given name. Non-human names, for such entities as corporations, are indexed just as they appear on the document. By statute the index entries must include the names of the parties and the book and page numbers or other information for finding specific pages. The index entry also will show the date that the instrument was registered; at least one name for another party to the instrument, known as a *reverse party*; an abbreviation for the type of document; and a brief description of the real estate based on information that appears in the document. To use the indexes, searchers must be familiar with the standards and local variations for the manner in which names are indexed, such as how names with punctuation are depicted, how complex names are grouped, and when and how abbreviations are used. Compounding the challenge is that real estate interests increasingly are created in unusual ways, transactions are less localized, and names are more diverse.

Although the rules for indexing are the same in each county, each county makes its own determination about many aspects of the index, such as whether a printed index will be available or only an index created by a computerized system. Computerized systems often are available on the Internet as well as at physical terminals within the office. System functionality includes features that suggest responses that may not match exactly, such as applying certain equivalencies for abbreviations, comparing without regard to spaces and punctuation, and providing some suggestions that sound the same but may not be identical letter-by-letter. Many who have no experience with register indexes would nonetheless be familiar with many of the search features because of their experience with standard Internet search engines. Registers and their deputies and

---

69. G.S. 161-22.3; Minimum Standards for Indexing Real Property Instruments, *available at* www.secretary.state.nc.us/land/ThePage.aspx.

70. G.S. 161-22(g).

assistants can provide guidance about available functions, but experience is always an advantage in navigating specialized systems, such as register of deeds indexes.

A few counties have replaced the traditional grantor–grantee index with a parcel identifier number (PIN) index. In this system, each parcel of land is assigned a unique identifier number (such as 9874058785), and all instruments affecting that parcel are indexed under that number. The numbers are graphically displayed on digital maps. This type of index in the register's office enables review of a chain of ownership for a particular parcel and is an essential part of an integrated land records system. But searchers typically supplement their search of the records by checking the name index system.

In a typical search of a name index system, the searcher will begin with the current owner's name and the recording information for the owner's deed. The examiner works backward using the grantee index until the chain of conveyances covers the search period, which typically will only go back about thirty years, a period considered sufficiently long for practical purposes. The owners' names will then be searched using the grantor index for deeds of trust and other rights that may have been conveyed during ownership. Each deed of trust will then be checked for records of satisfaction to determine whether they still apply. Plans will be reviewed for additional information. A search involving only a few owners and no complications may take an hour or two. Other records must also be checked for possible adverse claims, such as the tax records and court files. Confusion or complication is frequently encountered, and the project could take several hours or several days. Often the result is the need for a decision about whether an unresolved issue is sufficient risk for the buyer to withdraw or whether it can be addressed with an adjustment to the purchase price or title insurance. Sound decisions about how to handle complications most likely require expert legal advice.

3.8 Options and Rights of First Refusal

With the usual purchase agreement the buyer commits to a purchase if certain conditions are met. An *option* agreement gives someone a right but not an obligation to purchase or acquire an interest in property in exchange for an option payment or as part as a larger agreement. For example, a potential buyer could pay $1,000 for a right to purchase land that lasts for one year, during which the potential buyer will have tests done on the real estate, conduct a feasibility study, and seek development approvals with the owner's cooperation. The buyer can then buy the real estate by the deadline at a price described in the contract, either a fixed amount or according to a formula, such as at the appraised value or an amount for each lot that can be subdivided from the real estate. Option agreements can be structured in an infinite variety of ways to meet the parties' wishes. The buyer is not committing to a purchaser, and therefore these contracts are not subject to the same requirements as residential purchase agreements.

Options to purchase are sometimes included in leases, especially for commercial properties. In this kind of an arrangement the tenant is given a right to purchase the real estate at a fixed price, or at a price to be determined by some other means, if notice is given within a certain time before the end of the lease. An option clause should specify other essential terms for both the exercise of the option and the closing on the conveyance, including such things as whether a default under the lease extinguishes the option and what happens if the lease is extended.

A *right of first refusal* in real estate is a right given to someone to match an offer that the owner receives for the real estate. It is similar to an option in that it creates an option to purchase in the future but is different in that the terms for exercising the option will be determined by someone yet unknown. In the typical right of first refusal agreement, the owner must give a received offer to purchase to the holder of the right and the holder has a certain period within which to agree to purchase on the same price and other terms. Rights of first refusal tend to be more complicated and troublesome than they may first appear. Issues can arise about how exactly the holder's purchase must match the terms of the other offer that triggers the right. Other issues can arise about rights of inspection, financing contingencies, and a wide range of other contractual issues that may have different implications for the holder of the right and the party that made the offer. Also, the owner cannot offer the real estate outright for sale because anyone else who might want to buy the real estate must await the option holder's decision. This can cause other potential buyers to refrain from making offers.

3.9 Title Insurance

Most real estate sales now involve title insurance issued by one of the major national title insurance companies. Title insurance is a multibillion dollar industry. Title insurance companies range from local, family-owned agencies to international publicly traded corporations, including four major groups of insurers that have the vast majority of the market: First American, Fidelity, Stewart, and Old Republic. Homebuyers usually must pay for a policy as a condition of getting a mortgage loan. Unlike most forms of insurance, a premium is paid only once: when real estate is purchased or when a mortgage loan is obtained. An owner gets an *owner's policy*; a lender gets a *loan policy* that gives the lender protection in case the borrower does not have title to the real estate. When a title problem is covered by title insurance, the insurance company will step in to attempt to resolve it or will pay for the insured's lost real estate value as a result of it.

One reason that title insurance often goes unnoticed is that in a modern real estate conveyance its cost seems to blend into charges for loans, broker commissions, transfer taxes, and other closing expenses. Currently, a premium for an owner's policy is about $200 for the first $100,000 of coverage, with a lower per-thousand rate at higher amounts. An owner can get a policy at the same time as a loan policy for no additional premium. A policy can be obtained at a substantially lower rate for the same real estate and same coverage as a policy already issued to a previous owner by the same title insurance company. North Carolina title insurers all charge essentially the same rates because they may charge only rates that have been filed with the N.C. Insurance Commission, and they rely on a rating bureau to file for approved rates.[71] They can vary in the extent of coverage they are willing to give for the same rate. The agent who issues the policy keeps part of the premium paid by the buyer as a commission. The amount is an arrangement between the agent and the title insurance company.

Although, like any form of insurance, a title insurance policy gives certain protection against loss, it is fundamentally different in that essentially it prevents an owner or lender from having a problem by identifying the possibility that there could be one. A title insurance policy may be issued only if a lawyer approved by the title insurance company has done a reasonable title examination, which would involve examining the public records for possible title problems.[72] The owner or lender who is asking

---

71. G.S. 58-40-30; G.S. 58-40-40.
72. G.S. 58-26-1(a).

for the policy and learns of a problem can seek to correct the problem or renegotiate or terminate the purchase contract. The bottom line is that title insurance can protect buyers and lenders by making it more likely they will only have real estate free of serious title problems.

3.9.1 Coverage

In essence, title insurance protects against something that could have been found in the title examination but was not. But coverage is not limited to something that a reasonable title examination should have uncovered. It is accepted practice within the real estate transactional community to search title only back to a point in time, say within the last thirty years, on the assumption that it is very unlikely that a problem dating further back in the records would still exist. Title insurance therefore may protect against matters that even a reasonably careful title examination might have missed. It also protects the insured from hidden risks, such as forged deeds, conveyances that omitted entitled heirs, and unrecorded easements.

The owner's policy of title insurance covers the owner's title to the real estate described in Schedule A of the policy as of the date the policy was issued. Schedule A will be the same description as contained in the deed to the owner. Matters to which the premises are subject—such as restrictive covenants that burden the premises—will be listed as specific exceptions in Schedule B of the policy, and there is no insurance to protect against them.

The owner's policy covers four types of problems. First, coverage is provided if someone other than the insured owner has title to the real estate described in the policy. Second, the insured is covered against any defect in, or lien or encumbrance on, the title to the real estate. Third, the insured is covered if the title to the real estate is *unmarketable*. Title is considered to be unmarketable only if it is subject to title issues that create reasonable doubt for a reasonably prudent buyer. For example, a customary utility easement serving the premises will not cause marketability questions, but a road easement that crosses where it makes construction impossible would raise such questions. The fourth type of covered matter is a lack of a right of access to and from the land. This would be the case if a lot is surrounded by someone else's land and has no legal right to a path to cross it to get to the public road. The question is whether there is a right of access not whether it is the most convenient route or is expensive to maintain.

Home mortgage lenders typically do not require borrowers to have an owner's policy, but they do require a loan policy. The standard loan policy of title insurance covers a mortgagee against loss resulting from any of the four circumstances for which the owner's policy provides coverage. The loan policy also covers several additional circumstances. A loan policy insures against the invalidity or unenforceability of the insured mortgage lien. The mortgage lien, not the underlying debt, is insured. The policy provides no coverage against an insured's inability or refusal to pay. Title insurers also are more willing to cover some things for loan policies that they will not cover for owner's policies. A typical example of this is the exception for matters that only a survey would disclose; coverage for such matters may be available for loan policy based on some basic boundary information.

In addition to the basic coverage of owner's and loan policies, insurers offer coverage for certain other matters by means of *endorsements*. For a home buyer, these are likely to be involved only when required by the mortgage lender. There are different types of endorsements for residential lenders and commercial lenders and owners. Some endorsements can be obtained without additional charge; others can be obtained only for an additional charge, though in many cases the charge is insubstantial. Several common endorsements are available for residential loans, which provide coverage to meet the demands of the secondary mortgage market. A standard secondary mortgage market endorsement provides coverage against easements that adversely affect residential use; violations of listed restrictions, covenants, and conditions; and discrepancies, conflicts in boundary lines, and encroachments that an accurate survey would disclose. This applies only to a loan policy. A condominium endorsement provides coverage for compliance with the condominium statutes, the status of charges and assessments, and the other matters that are special to condominium units. Many different kinds of endorsements are available in the commercial real estate context. Some require survey reports and certifications, and affidavits from parties in possession. Such matters must be raised specifically with the title insurer.

3.9.2 Exclusions and Exceptions

Title insurance policies contain *exclusions* from coverage for a number of matters. These include the effect of building codes and land use laws, including environmental laws. No coverage is provided for losses resulting from governmental takings through the exercise of eminent domain, unless notice of the taking was recorded before the date of the policy. Another exclusion is for matters that the insured created or agreed to, such as if an owner allows a contractor's lien to be imposed by not making payments or if someone bought real estate knowing it was occupied or if the owner knew about a title problem and agreed to accept it.

Title insurance policies contain both standard and special *exceptions* to coverage. There are several standard exceptions. Exceptions are standardized or tailor-made limitations that apply only to some policies or particular premises. They are listed on Schedule B of the policy. Common exceptions involve boundary line conflicts, area shortages, or structures overlapping boundaries. Similarly, a policy will contain an exception for what only a survey would show—that is, what will not be evident from the recorded instruments. The typical situation to which the survey exception applies is a conflict due to mistaken distances in deeds. Another standard exception is for liens that arise in connection with construction, known as a *mechanic's lien* (discussed in Section 4.7.3). The title insurer may also list other specific matters that are detected, such as easement or restrictive covenants. In addition, if the title search reveals already conveyed interests, such as un-discharged mortgages or municipal tax liens, these will be listed as exceptions.

3.9.3 Claims

Even though the title insurance issuance process is intended to identify problems before closing, claims under the policy do arise. Hidden defects in title are the most common type of claim under a title insurance policy. This includes many kinds of errors in real estate descriptions, which may occur when the dimensions for subparts do not equal the dimensions for the tract from which they were subdivided. Claims also arise when an interest in the chain of title is missed, such as an easement.

When a claim is made an insurer will investigate the circumstances and assess what would be necessary to correct the problem. The insurer's duty is triggered by written notice, and prompt notice must be given. The event that requires notice may be someone filing litigation disputing title, or it may be some other form of notice of a dispute for which title insurance may provide coverage, such as a letter from a neighbor declaring ownership to real estate covered by the policy. When an insured party makes a claim, the title insurer has several options. It may cure the problem by obtaining a curative instrument or by taking other action that results in the insured having the title that had been expected. The insurer may choose to litigate to resolve the problem. The insurer also may pay compensation for loss or damage, which sometimes occurs instead of litigation and sometimes occurs after litigation has been unsuccessful. The insurer also may choose to pay the amount of insurance to the insured, which it will do if the defense is unlikely to succeed and the litigation costs will only increase the payments it expects to make. If the insurer pays the amount of insurance rather than defend, the insured owner or lender may still defend the title but without the insurer's financial support.

The policy amount is a contractual limit to the insurer's responsibility for covered losses. The policy limit for an owner's policy is the amount paid by the insured owner, sometimes automatically increased by a small percentage over time to account for anticipated inflation. The policy limit for a loan policy is the amount of the loan. A claim is likely to be made on a loan policy only after the loan has been default and the title problem prevents foreclosure, a rare circumstance. When losses are paid under the policy, the amount of insurance is reduced by that amount. Costs for lawyers' fees and expenses do not reduce the policy amount.

A title insurance company that has paid a claim may try to recover its payments from another responsible party with or without the permission of the insured. This means that there could be litigation against someone even though the insured would prefer not to take such action. Litigation entails substantial cost, and uncertain results, and insurance companies tend to take their losses rather than spend more to pursue recovery from another party.

3.10 Fire and Hazard Insurance

Fire and hazard (homeowner's) insurance protects owners against damage from fire, many other hazards to the property, and personal liability for certain kinds of accidents that occur on their property. North Carolina law does not require owners to have such coverage, but all banks and institutional lenders require it to protect the value in the real estate in case of foreclosure. Owners without insurance take a great risk of loss in case of fire or other disaster. Deeds of trust typically give the mortgage lender the right to purchase an insurance policy to cover the real estate if the owner does not provide proof of it and, in turn, to charge the owner for the premium.

Standard policies do not provide protection against floods or earthquakes; special insurance programs may provide such protection. In high-risk areas, along the beach, for example, insurance may be difficult to obtain. There are programs to make insurance available in some such circumstances. Flood insurance, for one, can be obtained through the federal government's National Flood Insurance Program. In a low- to moderate-risk area, the premium is several hundred dollars per year, with higher rates in flood-prone areas. Many insurance agents can arrange for this insurance. Owners can contact the North Carolina Department of Insurance for further information about such programs.

The most obvious kind of protection provided by the homeowner's policy is coverage to repair or replace a structure damaged by fire or other accident. Usually coverage is in the amount of market value or purchase price, but owners should look to have enough coverage to replace the structure at current prices. The policy also will provide coverage for other structures that have been identified to the company, such as a garage or shed. Personal property coverage will be in a maximum set amount for household contents and other belongings used, owned, or worn by household members. Expensive items, such as jewelry and antiques, may require additional premiums. Policies also cover necessary living expenses for a certain period if the home is so damaged that it cannot be used while it is being repaired.

Homeowner's policies are also important for personal liability coverage, which applies to claims made for injuries or property loss to others, including medical expenses, such as if someone is injured from a fall on the real estate. An example of a common type of claim covered by this insurance is a neighbor's child who is injured while playing on the homeowner's real estate. Homeowner's coverage does not apply to injuries of household members. It also does not cover risks from businesses operated on the real estate; separate coverage must be obtained for that. Endorsements may add to coverage described earlier in the policy or remove or change it.

The amount of the premium for the insurance will be based on numerous factors, including the value, age, and condition of the structures, the real estate location, policy coverage limits, deductibles, and extra coverage obtained through policy endorsements.

Policies require homeowners to provide information to the insurer about the property conditions and other matters on which the insurer bases the coverage and premium amounts. Intentional misrepresentations could result in the coverage becoming void, and someone who makes intentionally false misrepresentations to get insurance or to make a claim can be subject to civil and criminal liability. Coverage does not exist until the insurance company issues a policy or a temporary binder. Coverage is for a defined period, usually one year, and an insurance company can decide not to renew the policy but must give advance notice of this decision, which in general must be at least forty-five days before the policy expires.[73] A North Carolina statute provides that insurers may cancel a policy only for certain reasons, including nonpayment of a premium, willful failure by the insured to take reasonable steps to protect the real estate from damage, and material misrepresentation or nondisclosure of a material fact in obtaining the policy.[74]

In addition to reviewing the policy carefully to see what is covered, owners should study the exclusions in the policy to see what is *not* covered and the conditions for what must be done if there is damage or some other loss for which a claim is to be made. One important condition, for example, is the need to give the insurance company prompt notice when something has happened for which a claim will be made. Failure to give notice within a reasonable time can prevent the owner from later receiving payment if the delay was not for a good cause and the failure interfered with the insurer's ability to take action in connection with the claim.

3.11 Transfers at Death

Most real estate transfers are accomplished with a deed recorded with the register of deeds. However, many transfers of real estate interests occur as a result of a current owner's death, and in many cases no instrument is recorded with the register of deeds to mark this event. This section describes the most common ways in which real estate is transferred at death, the nature of the rights acquired in this way, and how they are determined.

3.11.1 Automatic Transfers

By law, when an owner of real estate dies, the title to the real estate instantly transfers. If title was held in a form of ownership that involves survivorship—joint tenancy or tenancy by the entireties—the survivor automatically becomes the owner. For example, if a husband and wife own real estate as tenants by the entireties and the husband dies, the wife automatically becomes sole owner of all that real estate. No deed or action of any court is needed for it to happen. Those looking at the title later will be able to

---

73. G.S. 58-41-20.
74. G.S. 58-41-15.

confirm the transfer by seeing the survivorship rights in the deed and a death certificate for one of the joint owners. If there is no such ownership involving an automatic survivor, the title will pass to someone not mentioned in the deed: the person's heirs. If there is a valid will, the title will go to the beneficiaries named in the will. This may not be determined until the will has been probated in court, but once this occurs the ownership transfer relates back to the time of death.[75] If there is no will, the heirs are determined by what is known as the *intestacy statutes* (summarized in Section 3.11.4).

3.11.2 Transfers by Will

A will is used to pass property onto someone of choice. The transfer is confirmed in a probate action in superior court. The clerk is the judge of probate and handles the probate of wills and the administration of estates. An entire estate will be the subject of a probate in North Carolina if the person died in this state. An *ancillary administration* is available for a decedent who has real estate in North Carolina but was not a resident of North Carolina at the time of death.

The deceased person's personal representative in the probate can be either an executor chosen by the person when there is a valid will or an administrator when there is no will. The personal representative may have power to sell the property if this is what is specified in the will or if it is necessary to meet the decedent's debts and otherwise distribute the estate assets according to the will. If a sale of the decedent's property is to occur within two years of death, notice must be given to the decedent's creditors, which enables them to object to the sale if the real estate is necessary to meet those debts.[76] If the sale occurs after notice but before the final account in the estate has been approved by the clerk of court, the personal representative must sign the deed along with the heirs of the estate.

A copy of the will is filed in the superior court when the probate is filed. Within three months after a personal representative has been appointed, the representative will file an inventory that lists all of the property owned by the decedent at the time of death. In general, a final accounting of the estate and how it has been distributed is to be filed within one year, subject to extensions for tax-filing obligations and other circumstances. Unless a will provides otherwise, the heirs will take the real estate subject to any

---

75. G.S. 28A-15-2; G.S. 31-39.
76. G.S. 28A-17-12.

existing deeds of trust or leases.[77] If the deceased person specified that the real estate was to pass free of these obligations, this will be allowed only if there are sufficient other assets in the estate to pay what is owed to creditors or as taxes.

A *transfer on death* deed, used in some states as a *will substitute*, through which an owner designates a beneficiary who acquires the property only upon the owner's death, is not recognized in the North Carolina statutes, and its effect is an unsettled question in this state.

3.11.3 Trusts

Real estate commonly passes from a deceased person as a result of a trust. A trust involves three parties. The person who created the trust and intends to put property into it is called the *settlor, grantor,* or *trust creator.* More than one person can create a single trust. The person to whom the property is transferred, and who agrees to follow the instructions given by the settlor, is the *trustee.* Sometimes there is more than one trustee. By statute a trustee must act prudently when administering a trust, exercising reasonable care, skill, and caution.[78] The person who receives the benefits of the trust, which can be periodic payments earned from the property or, upon a certain date or event, the property itself, is a *beneficiary.* There usually is more than one beneficiary, and some beneficiaries may have a contingent interest that takes effect only upon certain conditions, such as someone else's death.

Trusts are characterized as *testamentary* or *living.* A testamentary trust is created by will. Property will go into the trust upon the creator's death and be held by a trustee for some time, with the property to be later conveyed to the beneficiaries. Many trusts allow distributions from earnings on the trust property, with a final distribution at some point, such as when someone reaches a certain age. Certain kinds of trusts are used for their tax advantages. For example, a *marital trust* may be used to enable a spouse to take advantage of the federal tax deduction for property. The property is held after one spouse's death so that the other spouse receives payments while still alive, and the spouse who is still alive may be given powers to designate who will receive the property upon that spouse's death.

A living trust is created during the owner's lifetime. One common form of such is a *revocable living* or *inter vivos* ("between the living") trust. The trust creator's property is transferred to the trustee, often initially the trust

---

77. G.S. 28A-15-3.
78. G.S. 36C-8-804.

creator or the trust creator's spouse, who holds it until the creator's death. Someone is named as a successor trustee to step in after the initial trustee's death. The trust agreement will specify who receives the property after the creator's death. When the property goes to the beneficiaries, the trustee records a deed. An advantage of this type of trust is to allow for the transfer of the property to the beneficiaries upon death without having to go through probate court.

3.11.4 Distribution without a Will

According to North Carolina law known as the *intestacy statutes*,[79] if a person owning real estate dies without a will and has a living spouse, the surviving spouse has a right to no less than a one-third interest in the real estate. If the deceased left no children or other lineal descendants, such as grandchildren, the spouse will inherit all of the real estate. If there is only one child or lineal descendant, the spouse will take one-half. Similarly, if there is no child or lineal descendant but there is at least one parent, the spouse takes one-half. If there is more than one child or lineal descendant, the spouse takes one-third. The statutes also give a surviving spouse the option to choose a right to live on the property during life rather than receive a share of the ownership.[80] If there is no spouse and no lineal descendant, the estate goes to the parents; if there also is no parent, the estate goes to siblings, including the lineal descendants of a deceased sibling. If there also are no siblings, the statute then provides for distribution in shares to grandparents and in the lines of aunts and uncles.

As among the individuals who share, the law in North Carolina divides the shares into branches, and the individuals at the same level of the branch divide up the branch's share.[81] For example, if there is a spouse, one child, and two grandchildren of a deceased child, there are three branches. The spouse would take one-third and the child one-third, and the grandchildren of the deceased child would each take one-half of a branch, or, one-sixth of the shares.

The statutes also address how the share is calculated when the parties were in the process of being divorced and an equitable distribution is awarded subsequent to the death of a spouse.

---

79. G.S. 29-14; G.S. 29-15.
80. G.S. 29-30.
81. G.S. 29-16.

3.12 Seller and Buyer Liability

The vast majority of real estate transfers are completed successfully without anyone considering a lawsuit. Even when problems or disagreements arise, the parties usually are able to compromise with a financial adjustment or other accommodation. Even if this means someone gets or gives more than expected, avoiding litigation is usually the better course. Legal disputes, and especially litigation, are upsetting, time-consuming, and expensive, and almost always the outcome is unpredictable. Nonetheless, disputes often do arise, and court action sometimes becomes the means of resolving them. The following describes the most common kinds of the claims and the remedies that the law affords for real estate disputes involving transfers.

3.12.1 Common Claims

There are two types of situations that most commonly result in lawsuits over real estate transfers: breach of the purchase contract and misrepresentation.

3.12.1.1 *Breach of Contract*

A buyer could be liable for breach of contract for refusing to close without having a right to do so. For instance, most contracts allow the buyer to withdrawal if financing cannot be obtained. But the contract also requires the buyer to apply for financing and to give notice to the seller by a certain date if it cannot be arranged. The buyer cannot simply sit idly by as the deadline passes without being liable for breach of contract. Similarly, a buyer's claim based on contract will be the result of something the seller promised but failed to do. The most likely reason why a seller would be in breach of contract would be if the seller reneges and decides to keep the real estate or sell it to someone else.

Not every violation of a contract creates a legal claim. Parties must act in good faith to satisfy conditions. As described in Section 3.2 above, a failure to meet a deadline likely is not a sufficient breach of a contract to warrant liability unless the contract made very clear that the deadline was strict. The breach must be *material* for it to raise the possibility of a claim. For example, if the seller lists the real estate as having 2,400 square feet and it actually has 2,350 square feet, the difference is unlikely to be seen as important enough to be the basis for liability.

3.12.1.2 *Fraud and Misrepresentation*

The second common claim against a seller in connection with the purchase of real estate is for fraud or misrepresentation. (A seller's responsibility in connection with required structural disclosures is discussed in Section 3.2.2.) In general, a seller is not responsible for defects in the real estate unless the contract provides a warranty or the seller has told the buyer something that is false knowing that the buyer was relying on it. Someone selling a home is not deemed to make implied promises about the condition of real estate improvements. The same is not true for new construction. A builder gives an implied warranty that new construction is done in a proper worker-like manner. This includes protection against major defects in the structure and major systems, which must be built according to the customary standard of quality in the industry. The builder's implied warranty protects against hidden defects; it does not apply to defects that a reasonable buyer would have seen upon inspection.[82] Therefore, a buyer who knows of a problem and completes the purchase without objection cannot later sue the builder based on the implied warranty. The time limit on a claim based on this rule is ten years.[83] The builder and buyer can override the implication of what is warranted by agreeing to different warranties or clearly agreeing that there are none.

Contrary to popular misconception, fraud cases are uncommon. Fraud involves something much more than someone's failure to do more to prevent a bad situation. It involves specific acts intended to deceive, and this is difficult to prove. There are several factors that someone must prove in addition to harm caused by a false statement or a failure to say something under circumstances that equate to a false statement. The person accused of fraud must have misrepresented a fact that is *material* to the transaction, which means it must be important and not inconsequential. The misrepresented fact must be specific, not something vague. The person who made the misrepresentation must have either known it was false or have remained intentionally ignorant of it in a way intended to be harmful. That person must also have intended for the harmed person to rely on the misrepresentation.[84]

Most successful fraud claims involve elaborate schemes. When fraud can be proved, the party harmed by it may be able to recover substantial damages not available for ordinary breach of contract claims if the conduct was a reckless and wanton disregard of the harmed party's rights.

---

82. Griffin v. Wheeler-Leonard & Co., 290 N.C. 185, 202, 225 S.E. 2d 557, 566–67 (1976); Hartley v. Ballou, 286 N.C. 51, 61–62, 209 S.E.2d 776, 783 (1974).

83. G.S. 1-52(16).

84. Powell v. Wold, 88 N.C. App. 61, 63–64, 362 S.E.2d 796, 797 (1986).

A more common claim that is related to fraud is *negligent misrepresentation*. This is a claim similar to fraud, but it does not require the same degree of proof about intent to deceive. Someone who provides information in business transactions can be liable if the intended recipient was harmed by reasonably relying upon it, and the person making the misrepresentation acted unreasonably in obtaining and communicating the information (see Section 3.3.5 regarding brokers).[85]

Fraud and misrepresentation claims most commonly arise regarding property conditions. Buyers have a duty to be diligent and arrange for reasonable inspections. Sellers will not be liable for conditions about which no information was volunteered and that buyers could observe themselves or with a reasonable inspection. Also, not every bit of information provided is a basis for a claim. Sellers commonly provide information about the real estate that is preliminary. Saying "I haven't had any problems with the roof" is not the same as giving a warranty that the roof is as good as new.

A buyer's responsibility to look into possible problems is heightened when there are signs they exist. For example, in one case, a court held that a buyer could not sue the seller for nondisclosure of a leak problem when the buyer's home inspection report warned her of a possible water problem and advised her to have a roofing contractor look at it but she declined to do so.[86] A buyer likely cannot hold the seller accountable if the buyer decided not to have an inspection that otherwise would be considered an ordinary step in self-protection. But courts have found a possible case of misrepresentation when the seller knew of a problem and seemingly tricked the buyer into not investigating the possibility. For example, in one case a seller had information based on a soil investigation that the land would not support a septic system. On the disclosure form given to the buyer, the seller crossed out the space for this information and sold the real estate "as is" in the contract. The seller also told the buyers that the land was of a nature to support a septic system, giving the false impression that a favorable test had been done and leading the buyer to conclude that there was no need for another test. The court held that this could be fraud.[87]

---

85. *Id.* at 67–68, 362 S.E.2d at 799.
86. MacFadden v. Louf, 182 N.C. App. 745, 643 S.E.2d 432 (2007).
87. Little v. Stogner, 162 N.C. App. 25, 592 S.E.2d 5 (2004).

3.12.2 Remedies

If someone breaches a promise in a purchase agreement, the rights that the other party has depends both on the terms of the contract and the law of damages. Four basic remedies are potentially available to a party faced with a breach of a purchase agreement: compelling performance, rescission, liquidated damages, and damages. The availability of any particular remedy depends on the circumstances.

3.12.2.1 *Compelled Purchase or Sale*

When a purchase agreement is breached, a court order to compel a closing may seem an obvious remedy. For a buyer, this means compelling the seller to convey for the purchase price, and for a seller this means compelling the buyer to pay the purchase price and accept the conveyance. This kind of a court-compelled relief is called *specific performance.*

Specific performance is not a usual remedy for an ordinary breach of contract, but a real estate purchase contract can be an exception to this general rule. When courts have ordered specific performance in real estate cases it has been because every piece of real estate is seen as unique and payment of money damages, if any, is seen as an inadequate remedy. Of course there must be a valid, enforceable contract in existence for specific performance to be available. Buyers will be entitled to specific performance only if they are able to show that they have fully performed their part of the bargain or are ready, willing, and able to do so.[88] Specific performance is unlikely to be awarded to a seller if the real estate can be sold to someone else, in which case the seller's remedy would be the difference between a fair price for such a sale and what the buyer had promised to pay.

3.12.2.2 *Re-Conveying*

A buyer who paid for a deed under circumstances in which there was fraud or intentional misrepresentation may seek to *rescind* the transaction by returning the real estate in exchange for a refund. For example, in one case a court said that rescission was a possible remedy when a seller's broker led a buyer to believe that the seller's property included a large tract that the broker knew or should have known was not part of it.[89] Rescission is intended to put the parties back in the position they were in before the

---

88. Munchak Corp. v. Caldwell, 301 N.C. 689, 694, 273 S.E.2d 281, 285 (1981); Mizell v. Greensboro Jaycees, 105 N.C. App. 284, 289, 412 S.E.2d 904, 908 (1992).
89. Howell v. Waters, 82 N.C. App. 481, 347 S.E.2d 65 (1986).

conveyance. Consequently, a buyer cannot get rescission unless the buyer comes to court within a reasonable time and before the seller's position has changed so that rescission becomes impossible or terribly unfair. Subject to general principles of equity, a buyer allowed to rescind must return any benefits received prior to rescission but may also be allowed to offset the value of any improvements that the buyer has made.

3.12.2.3 Liquidated Damages

As described in Section 3.2.3, the typical real estate purchase contract requires the buyer to make an *earnest money deposit*. Typically the contract provides that if the buyer breaches the contract the deposit is forfeited to the seller. In this situation, the contract is likely to be interpreted as substituting the deposit amount for precisely calculated money damages but leaving open the possibility of other remedies. The forfeiture of a deposit is what is called *liquidated damages*, which means a specific amount set in advance. Some liquidated damages clauses provide that retention of the deposit is the only remedy, not an optional one. Regardless of whether the clause is stated as optional or exclusive, it will be enforced only when it meets a reasonableness standard applied by the courts.

North Carolina courts generally recognize and will enforce the parties' freedom to agree in a contract about what the damages will be if someone breaches. As the N.C. Supreme Court said, "[T]he parties, being informed as to the facts and circumstances, are better able than anyone else to determine what would be a fair and reasonable compensation for a breach; but the courts have been greatly influenced by the fact that in almost all the cases the damages are uncertain and very difficult to estimate."[90] But this view assumes that the parties are making a reasonable effort to set an amount in the contract rather than leave it until later to try to figure out the actual amount of loss.[91] Courts are not receptive to enforcing unreasonable amounts that are considered to be a penalty unconnected to anticipated loss, especially when one of the parties seems to have taken advantage of an unsophisticated party that did not understand the provision. The burden is on the party attempting to avoid the provision to prove that it meets these legal requirements.

---

90. Knutton v. Cofield, 273 N.C. 355, 361, 160 S.E.2d 29, 34–35 (1968) (quoting Bradshaw v. Millikin, 173 N.C. 432, 435, 92 S.E. 161, 163 (1917)).

91. E. Carolina Internal Med., P.A. v. Faidas, 149 N.C. App. 940, 945–46, 564 S.E.2d 53, 56 (2002).

3.12.2.4 Damages Based on Actual Loss

If a party is not limited to a set damage remedy in the contract, the party harmed by another's breach may recover contract damages. For a seller, the measure is the difference between the contract price and the actual value of the real estate at the time of the breach. This could result in no award if the market value of the real estate at the time of the breach is equal to or greater than the contract price. The seller has the burden of proving the values to establish a loss.

A seller also may be able to recover what are known as *consequential damages*. These may include relatively minor expenses, such as deed preparation costs, but also potentially large liabilities for brokerage commissions. As discussed in Section 3.3.4, brokers can sometimes be entitled to commissions even if there is no closing, and this could be a consequential damage to the seller. To be recoverable these kinds of expenses must be something that the party who breached the contract would normally expect to be incurred as a result of the breach. Extraordinary or very unusual expenses are not recoverable.

A buyer may suffer damages if a seller refuses to convey. A buyer could be entitled to repayment of expenses incurred, such as title search costs, loan application fees, and inspection charges. A buyer may also be entitled to recover damages equal to the difference between the price for which the seller agreed to sell and the market value at the time of the breach, which is likely to be a factor only in a market with rapidly rising prices. According to the general rules of damages, lost profits, such as gain from resale of the real estate, could be recoverable only if they were reasonably certain and foreseeable to the seller, which usually is not the case. When the real estate conveyed to a buyer turns out to be less than represented and there is a basis for recovery (see Sections 3.12.1.1–2), the measure of damages is the difference between the actual value of what the buyer received and the actual value of what was represented.

4 Financing

Real estate ownership is tied to the willingness of banks and other financial institutions to make substantial loans. Few homeowners have enough savings to purchase real estate without getting a loan. Enterprises also depend on real estate financing. Developers, shopping center and apartment owners, and industrial enterprises use complex loan structures to pay for the construction, operation, and upgrade of their properties. These various borrowers rely on bankers, brokers, and lawyers to explain the different loan products that are available and the rights being given to lenders as security for repayment in the form of deeds of trust and other agreements. The complexity of these arrangements cannot be summarized in a few pages in this book. This chapter is intended as an introduction to the basic concepts of mortgage lending and deeds of trust and their foreclosure. Professional advice should be obtained both as to the specifics of a suitable arrangement and how to proceed if difficulties arise.

4.1 Secured Financing and Equity

Real estate purchase and ownership almost always involves financing by a bank or other institutional lender. The legal relationship between the borrower and the lender involves two basic agreements. Under one, the borrower agrees to repay the lender on a specified schedule and with specified interest; this agreement usually is documented in the form of a *promissory note*. Under the other, the borrower conveys to the lender a right to foreclose if payment is not made as promised; in North Carolina, this agreement usually is in the form of a deed of trust. A *deed of trust* is functionally the same thing as a *mortgage* (the more common term in many other states), and, in home financing, a loan that is subject to a deed of trust or mortgage is commonly referred to simply as a mortgage or a mortgage loan. There are many other real estate financing arrangements, some of which are complex, especially for construction projects and commercial properties. The following provides an overview of the basics of the most common arrangements.

As everyone knows, someone may be willing to loan some money in exchange for nothing more than a promise to repay. There is always the risk of nonpayment, either because the borrower breaks the promise or suffers financial losses and becomes unable to pay. The lender may be willing to take the risk of being unable to collect, especially if the loan is small or is being made to a family member.

As an incentive for many lenders to make a substantial loan with greater risk, the borrower may promise to pay more than the loan by adding interest, usually equal to a percentage of the loan. Interest compensates the lender for risk and for not having the loan amount available for other purposes, whether for purchasing something or investing it. For example, in simple form the agreement could be to pay 5 percent interest on $1,000 loaned for one year for a total of $1,050. Also, as a further incentive to pay on time, the agreement may call for interest to continue to be added and for the rate to go up after the due date.

In lending terms *security* is a lender's right to sell the borrower's property to collect a loan, as occurs with a deed of trust. With an *unsecured* loan, the lender bases the decision to make the loan solely on an assessment of the borrower's likelihood of repayment and the profit that the lender can expect by collecting interest. If the borrower does not repay, the lender can sue and try to attach the borrower's other assets. With an unsecured loan the lender has no right to the borrower's assets without litigation and no priority over any other creditor. For these reasons, unsecured loans are rarely available for the purchase of real estate. Instead, real estate loans usually are *secured* and the lender has a right to sell the real estate at foreclosure to collect. Any property or right can be used as security; the most common form is real estate.

Lenders are willing to loan large amounts of money for real estate purchases and development because real estate has substantial value that can be fairly reliably estimated based on market information. Also, historically real estate values have been assumed to increase over time, which means that the lender's protection can be expected to increase as the value rises and the loan balance decreases as it is paid down. As recent events have shown, however, this assumption can be wrong, and when it is, real estate lending and borrowing decisions turn out to have involved more risk than had been thought. But when lenders are confident that the value of real estate is greater than the amount of the loan and will stay that way, lenders are willing to loan large sums of money for a long time. They are also willing to accept lower interest rates than would be required for an unsecured loan. Home mortgages lenders may be willing to wait as long as thirty years for repayment, while most unsecured loans are not made for a term of more than a couple of years and at interest rates several percentage points higher than that of secured loans.

A lender's sound decision to make a mortgage loan to any particular borrower is based on a combination of factors, including the value of the real estate and the borrower's capacity to pay. Lenders want to be able to recover the full loan amount plus expenses if the borrower stops paying and the real estate must be sold at foreclosure. Under normal circumstances, the amount that can be obtained at a foreclosure sale will be less than the price that would be obtained in an ordinary sale by the owner. There may be less opportunity for marketing and negotiation with foreclosure, and buyers at foreclosure tend to factor in a discount for problems that could arise at a forced sale that are not expected with purchases directly from an owner. Taking into account historic practices, most lenders typically are willing to loan up to eighty percent of the current appraised value of the real estate, wanting the remaining twenty percent as a cushion to ensure full recovery.

Obviously a real estate owner also cares about the relationship between real estate value and loan amount. A lender may effectively control real estate through a deed of trust, but to the borrower the real estate is a home as well as an investment. If a foreclosure occurs soon after purchase, the owner will lose the real estate and probably not be able to get back the deposit and purchase costs. And as the value of the real estate increases and the loan amount decreases, the owner's investment value in the real estate increases. This difference between what is owed and what the real estate is worth is known as *equity*. Most owners purchase real estate expecting their equity to increase. As equity increases, it also becomes available as a means for getting additional loans. Increased equity may enable the owner to pay off the prior loan and get more money for other purposes, such as home improvements or other purchases. Owners also can get additional money without paying off the prior loan by getting what is known as a *home equity loan* or *second mortgage*. A lender making a home equity loan is protected only to the extent that the value of the home is greater than the amount secured by the prior, first mortgage. Because such a lender's risk is greater than for the first mortgage, the interest rate for the second priority loan may be higher and the term for repayment shorter.

Contrary to lenders' and borrowers' expectations, real estate values sometimes go down rather than up. If the value decreases to less than the remaining loan amount, the loan is considered to be *underwater* or *short*. The loan becomes unsecured to this extent, and it presents a problem for both the lender and the borrower. The lender may no longer be able to expect to recover the full loan amount if there is a foreclosure. Although the lender may have the right to sue the borrower to recover the difference, this is a costly and uncertain prospect. Of course the borrower also faces difficulty, primarily an inability to sell the real estate because the market price will not bring in enough money to pay off the loan. Mortgage loans do not go away just because real estate is sold; the sale probably triggers the lender's right to foreclose and sell the property to pay off the loan.

This balance between real estate value and loans can have a serious impact not only on particular borrowers but also on local economies. One of the main reasons for the severe financial downturn in 2008 was that the values of many properties had been grossly overestimated, either by lack of careful appraisal or market downturns. When the prices that could be obtained for properties dropped, many lenders lost the ability to recover their loans, and borrowers lost their ability to sell their properties or pay off their loans. Most lenders have since become much more cautious in their estimates of real estate values and in their structuring of loans to ensure they can be repaid. Borrowers with limited means may have more difficulty getting loans than before, but they also are less likely to take on more than they can handle.

For those who have regular income or other substantial financial resources, mortgage loans are widely available from banks, savings and loans, and credit unions, among other places. A wide variety of loan arrangements are possible. A small percentage of homes are bought with what is known as *seller financing* or a *take-back loan*. Rather than obtain a loan from a lending institution, the buyer borrowers the purchase price from the seller, with a deed of trust or mortgage given to secure the repayment. This arrangement is likely to occur when the buyer and seller have a relationship, such as family members, and they see private financing as a way to avoid the costs and interests rates charged by institutional lenders. Sometimes it results from the buyer being unable to qualify for a loan from another lender. Among the risks of this kind of arrangement are improper documentation of the sale and thereby the creation of an unenforceable deed of trust or mortgage, the problem of ensuring that payments are made on time and dealing with calculating penalties, the difficulties and costs of foreclosure or legal action if the buyer defaults, and the severe impact that nonpayment may have on an individual seller.

In North Carolina the usual form of security interest is a deed of trust. Security interests can be created in any other type of property as well. This commonly occurs with commercial real estate. For example, some types of real estate are valuable for the rents that can be collected from tenants, such as apartment buildings and shopping centers. Lenders who make loans to owners of such properties not only want the ability to foreclose and sell the real estate upon a default, but they also want to be able to collect the rents and apply them to the loan balance. After the owner has stopped making payments on the loan it will take weeks or months before a foreclosure can be completed and the real estate can be sold to someone who can take the owner's place and collect the rents as owner–landlord. In the meanwhile, the lender wants to be able to collect the rents rather than have them continue to be paid to the defaulting owner. To establish a clear legal right to collect the rents that are owed to a defaulting owner–landlord, the lender uses an *assignment of leases and rents*. This kind of security instrument grants an owner's creditor a right to collect rents from the owner's tenants upon the owner's default. Often this right is included in a deed of trust. It may also be part of a separately recorded security instrument.

4.2 Payment Terms

Although competing lenders tend to offer similar mortgage rates, even slight differences can have significant financial implications. When choosing among available options borrowers should carefully examine all details about rates, length of payment, up-front costs, and other fees and charges. This analysis should include the total amount of financing charges over the lifetime of a loan.

Obviously, a primary consideration in understanding the cost of a loan is the interest rate. Interest rates vary depending on the length of the loan, and available rates change over time in reaction to economic trends. But interest is not the only factor. Most mortgage loans also involve significant initial costs. Often a borrower is charged *points* when the loan is made. A point is one percent of the loan amount. Similarly, loans often involve an *origination fee*, that is, a flat amount the lender charges. Costs added to the loan when it is made also may include substantial amounts for such routine matters as fees for title search, title insurance, and instrument recording as well as charges associated with loan approval, such as a fee for a credit report and a real estate appraisal. Lenders are often willing to advance these costs to the borrower by adding them to the principal amount of the loan. This is helpful to borrowers who do not have cash on hand to pay these costs at closing, but such a loan actually might be more expensive over the long run because closing costs are added to the principal on which interest is charged. All costs must be taken into account to properly compare available loans and to assess their affordability. Toward this end, federal law requires that all these costs be disclosed to the borrower (as described in Section 4.4).

Borrowers should also include in their affordability calculation other payments required in connection with ownership of the real estate. Among these ownership costs are taxes and insurance premiums. Lenders may insist on payment arrangements for these necessities. Insurance is important for protecting the value of the real estate, as it provides security for the loan. Without it, a fire or disaster could leave a lender unable to foreclose and receive enough to pay off the loan. A lender also wants protection against the possibility that a tax lien will cause a municipality to sell the real estate for a tax debt. To accomplish these objectives, most residential mortgage lenders require borrowers to make regular deposits into *escrow accounts* for payment of insurance premiums and taxes. These deposits are added to the monthly payment of principal and interest. The deposits are accumulated, and payments are made for insurance and taxes. The required amount of the deposit is adjusted as insurance and tax rates change. With an escrow, owners have the convenience of someone else managing the account. But regardless of their agreement with the lender, owners are responsible for paying taxes and insurance and so should keep track of these payments to ensure that they are correct and being made on time. Whatever the payment arrangement, owners need to take these amounts into account when considering the full cost of homeownership.

When considering the main part of the loan obligation, the borrower needs to understand the interest rate, how it is applied, and the schedule for payment. The *principal* is the amount the lender either gives to the borrower or pays on the borrower's behalf and is also known simply as the *loan amount.* As noted above, this may have various components in addition to what is paid to the seller as all or part of the purchase price. The borrower will repay this principal with interest.

Interest can be calculated in various ways. Simple interest is a percentage applied to the loan balance, or *outstanding principal.* Some personal loans use this method. More commonly, interest is compounded, with the percentage applied to both the principal and accrued interest. Savings accounts usually have compounded interest. Mortgage loans usually use *amortized* interest. This method allocates payments to interest and principal so that installments are equal during the payment term. As the principal amount goes down, the amount of interest calculated on that amount also goes down, and with each payment the balance shifts to less interest and more principal. The allocation of principal and interest for any given amount, term, and interest rate can be seen in an amortization schedule that is readily available on the Internet.

For example, if an owner borrows $100,000 at 6 percent interest on a loan to be repaid over thirty years, amortized payments will be just under $600 per month. The first month, $500 will go to interest. The high proportion of interest in this payment is due to the percentage being applied to the full amount of the principal: $100,000. Only about $100 will go to the principal, which reduces the balance only slightly. The total amount of the principal will decrease slowly during the first few years but more rapidly in later years, until at the end of thirty years, when almost the entire amount of the monthly payment is being applied to principal. An important point to understand is that in the early years of an amortized loan the principal decreases slowly and most of each payment goes to interest. This may have a tax advantage for the homeowner, who may be able to deduct the interest from income taxes. But it also means that a lot of interest is being paid. For the loan just described, at the end of thirty years more than $115,000 in interest will have been paid. For a $100,000 loan, the owner will ultimately pay a total of $215,000, though the total effect of the higher amount will be offset to the extent that interest was a tax deduction.

The total amount of interest paid is also a factor of the length of the loan. For example, if the borrower gets a fifteen-year loan at the same 6 percent interest rate as for the thirty-year loan described above, the monthly payments will be higher: about $844. However, the loan will be repaid in half the time and the total amount of interest that will have been paid will be under $52,000, less than half the total interest paid on a thirty-year loan.

The total interest paid over the lifetime of a loan also can be reduced if the borrower makes additional payments of principal without penalty. For example, if the borrower of the thirty-year loan described above makes additional $100 per month payments along with the $600 required, the $100 payment will lower the principal and therefore the interest, and the portion of the required payment applied to principal will accelerate more quickly. With this additional payment scenario, the loan will be paid off ten years early with a savings of almost $40,000 in interest.

The impact of amortization can be significant even with only a slight variation in interest rate. For example, for a thirty-year, $100,000 loan at 5 percent interest the monthly payment will be about $537. A 4.5 percent interest rate, meanwhile, will result in a monthly payment of about $507 or $30 less. This may not seem like much, but over the length of the loan, the borrower will pay $10,700 less in interest under the lower rate. Few borrowers take advantage of prepayment without penalty even though it is a standard feature in home loans.

A loan is called a *fixed loan* when the interest rate remains the same for the lifetime of the loan. Most loans are fixed loans. A feature included in some fixed loan arrangements is a *balloon payment*. Monthly installments are calculated as if the loan is amortized, but then, on a certain date, a payment of the full amount of the remaining principal is owed. For example, for the first seven years of a $100,000 loan, the borrower will make monthly installments based on a thirty-year amortization schedule with a balloon payment of the remaining principal and interest due at the end of that time period. At 6 percent interest, the monthly payments for seven years would be about $600, and the balloon payment would be more than $89,000. With this kind of payment schedule, the borrower either will have to refinance at seven years or pay the balloon off with other resources.

These calculations are based on the interest rate remaining the same throughout the lifetime of the loan. Mortgage interest rates go up or down depending on market conditions, including inflation rates and national credit policies. The changes that occur in these conditions over time make the loan a better or worse deal with respect to other loans. If a loan is made when interest rates are low and rates rise, the borrower has a good deal and the lender will be servicing a loan that may no longer be profitable. If a loan is made before interest rates decline, the lender has a profitable loan and the borrower is paying more than the market would require. In this situation the borrower is likely to refinance and pay off the higher interest rate loan.

Variable or *adjustable* rate loans take into account the likelihood of market changes and equalize the risks to both the lender and borrower. Lenders may be willing to offer a rate that initially is lower than a fixed rate in exchange for allowing the rate to go up as market rates go up. Adjustable rate loans have interest rates tied to various indexes of market rates, such as the London Interbank Offered Rate (LIBOR) or the U.S. federal funds rate. These indexes are for rates charged for loans to banks and not borrowers, so the rate that the borrower pays is likely to be two to three percent higher than the index rate. This added amount is known as the *margin.*

Adjustable rate loan arrangements have a number of other features that affect actual payment amounts. These include the adjustment period that sets how often the rate will change, which may range from six months to five years. This affects how quickly someone gets the advantage or disadvantage of changing rates. Also, rate caps limit how much the interest rate can change during any one period or over the course of the loan. All of these factors must be considered in comparing available loan options. Whether a fixed or variable rate loan is a better choice depends not only on these details but also on the mortgage markets, which are highly unpredictable.

These loan scenarios are based on a single disbursement of the loan amount. Some loans involve *future advances* in which the lender extends additional principal amounts over time. The loan likely will have a maximum total. When additional principal is advanced, the payment amount is recalculated. Loans can be extended also by making money available intermittently rather than by disbursing it at one time. With a *line of credit*, a lender agrees that as long as certain conditions are met the borrower can draw out money up to a maximum amount. The repayment terms can vary, including monthly payments of principal and interest or interest-only payments with a balloon of the entire payment and accrued interest on a certain date. Lines of credit are often used in commercial and construction loans and for home improvements, the borrower receiving money as actual expenses are incurred.

4.3 Loan Qualification

Institutional lenders are in the business of making loans. They want to attract borrowers and loan money to them. But their business also depends on borrowers being able to repay their loans. To maximize the likelihood of repayment, lenders analyze a number of aspects of a loan application, including the amount of the loan, the value of the property being offered as collateral, and the borrower's financial circumstances and credit history.

4.3.1 Home Loans

The availability of homeowner financing is important to both the buyer and the seller as well as to others involved in the transaction, such as real estate brokers. As noted in Chapter 3, purchase contracts usually are contingent on the buyer's ability to get financing. Even before entering into a contract, sellers may want assurance that financing will be available to avoid the risk of tying up the real estate with a buyer who has no reasonable likelihood of being able to get a loan. When there is reasonable doubt about the buyer's ability to get a loan, the seller may ask to see a *prequalification letter.* This is nothing more than a calculation performed by a lender based on information that the borrower provides about current income, debts, down payment, and requested loan amount. The letter is not an assurance that a loan actually will be made. An additional step in the process is known as *preapproval*, which also is based on basic information the borrower provides, but the information is verified to a limited degree by review of some documentation, such as a W-2 showing earnings and a bank statement showing money for the down payment. This too is not an assurance that a loan will be made. It is a tentative prediction based on partial information.

The formal loan approval process involves collection and review of a lot of verifiable information. A commonly used residential loan application form is Form 1003, (or ten-oh-three), which is used by the Federal National Mortgage Association (Fannie Mae). It is several pages long and requires information about the type of mortgage and terms requested; the real estate and the purpose of the loan; the borrower's employment, monthly income, housing expenses, and assets and liabilities; and the details of the proposed transaction. Most institutions use an automated system that analyzes the information provided by the borrower and makes a preliminary determination about the loan. The loan decision process is sometimes called *underwriting.* Usually no loan will be approved until this information is verified and other information is collected. Many of these next steps involve charges to the borrower, including a credit report and an appraisal of the value of the real estate. Even when the loan is approved based on this further information, the loan will be subject to conditions, including a satisfactory home inspection and title search. If these investigations reveal problems the lending institution may withdrawal the loan approval.

There are four main factors that lending institutions typically consider when they make lending decisions: the loan-to-value percentage, credit score, debt ratio, and financial reserves.

As described above, lenders rely on the value in real estate as security for their loans. The *loan-to-value (LTV) percentage* is the ratio of the loan amount to the real estate market value. The LTV percentage is important to the lender's assurance that if a foreclosure becomes necessary a sale of the real estate will result in proceeds that are enough to pay off the loan balance plus foreclosure costs. A common target for conventional loans is an LTV percentage of not more than eighty percent. In other words, the borrower must have cash saved for a deposit of at least twenty percent of the value of real estate. Higher LTV percentages (and lower deposit percentages) are commonly acceptable to lenders when there is some form of guarantee of payment, such as a veterans' program or other federal assistance program, and when the lender agrees to rely on private mortgage insurance, which is described below. The higher the LTV percentage, the more likely the lender will insist on escrow deposits of taxes and insurance. This is because foreclosure is more common on real estate loans made with higher LTV percentages.

The other main factors that lenders consider when making loan decisions involve the borrower's ability to pay. The calculations commonly used to assess this ability are the borrower's credit score, debt ratio, and financial reserves.

The *credit score* is obtained from a credit repository. The three most commonly used are TransUnion, Experian, and Equifax. These companies collect information about credit and payments from banks and merchants. Scores may differ among the companies but usually not significantly. The reports they provide show payment histories and scores that result from a formula of data, including types of credit used, how long it has been available, payment histories, and amounts owed. The score is highest for borrowers who have a history of a lot of credit and immediate payment. The scale is from 300 to 850 with most scores ranging between 600 and 800. A score in the 700s is likely to qualify a borrower for most kinds of loans.

The *debt ratio* is the percentage of a borrower's debt to the borrower's gross income (before taxes). A total debt ratio is based on payments for the requested mortgage loan plus other payments the borrower must make, such as for car loans. For example, a borrower who earns $36,000 per year, or $3,000 per month, and who proposes to pay $500 per month for a home loan and already pays $200 per month for a car loan would have a total debt ratio of $700 ($500 plus $200) to $3,000 or 23 percent. Generally lenders are most concerned when the ratio goes above forty percent. Doing some math using this forty percent limit, the borrower with a gross income of $36,000 per year and only $200 per month in other debt obligations might be approved for a mortgage loan of as much as $1,000. Although lenders may be willing to loan at these ratios, when payments consume a large part of the borrower's income there is serious risk of financial trouble if circumstances change negatively.

The third measure usually considered in the loan review process is the borrower's *financial reserves*. This is the value of the borrower's assets that could be used to pay the loan, such as savings accounts and mutual funds. Higher balances increase the lender's confidence in the borrower's ability to pay.

Ultimately the decision of a lender about any loan application depends on analysis of all of this information and a number of other factors, such as the lender's financial prospects. Borrowers must remember that a lender's decision to make a loan is not necessarily a reason to conclude that the loan is a sound financial decision. Even when a loan seems well within a lender's guidelines for sound lending practices, things can change, including the borrower's personal financial situation and the value of the real estate.

4.3.2 Mortgage Insurance

Lenders are sometimes willing to make a loan only if the borrower gets *mortgage insurance*. This requirement is a customary practice when the LTV percentage goes above eighty percent. Mortgage insurance gives lenders some protection against defaults. It is a contract with an insurance company that will reimburse a lender for losses if the lender is unable to recover payment in full from foreclosure on the real estate. If such insurance is available, lenders may be willing to loan more than the usual percentage of the real estate value.

A typical mortgage insurance premium for a $200,000 loan with an LTV percentage of ninety percent is about $500 per year. Mortgage insurance programs are available from government-funded agencies, such as the Federal Housing Administration (FHA), Farmers Home Administration (FmHA), and the Department of Veterans Affairs (VA). These programs are aimed at such individuals as veterans, farmers, and first-time homeowners, who have limited resources for down payments. There also are private mortgage insurers for other homeowners. Lenders that initially require mortgage insurance may be willing to lift the requirement once the LTV percentage passes a certain level after the principal has been paid down a significant amount.

4.3.3 Federal Programs for Residential and Small Farm Loans

Borrowers and lenders commonly engage various federal agencies and national organizations in connection with mortgage lending. Usually these institutions work behind the scenes, providing incentives or guaranties that allow lenders to make loans more accessible to homeowners with limited resources. They also package mortgages into investments that attract funds for lending purposes. Although distinguishing among these various institutions can be confusing and most likely is not necessary, their names are well known. Descriptions of the most commonly used lending institutions immediately follow.

4.3.3.1 U.S. Department of Veterans Affairs (VA)

The VA guarantees hundreds of thousands of mortgage loans each year for active duty military personnel, certain reservists and National Guard members, veterans, and their spouses. VA loans often have terms more favorable than are generally available because the VA gives the lender protection against a default with a guaranty (explained in Section 4.6.1). With a VA-guaranteed loan, an eligible person may be able to buy a home without a down payment or private mortgage insurance, and the rules limit fees and costs that qualifying lenders may charge.

4.3.3.2 Federal Housing Administration (FHA)

The largest insurer of mortgages in the world, the FHA insures lenders against borrower defaults for mortgages on single-family and multifamily homes, including manufactured housing. This encourages lenders to make loans to a greater number of potential homeowners. With an FHA loan, a borrower is able to get a mortgage with less money down than is ordinarily required, and the borrower obtains and pays for mortgage insurance through the FHA. These insurance payments are used to fund FHA programs.

4.3.3.3 *Federal National Mortgage Association (FNMA: Fannie Mae)*

Fannie Mae purchases mortgages and issues mortgage-related securities to make funds available to financial institutions and to support affordable rental housing programs. When an institution such as Fannie Mae purchases loans from banks, the banks then have funds for making other loans.

4.3.3.4 *Government National Mortgage Association (GNMA: Ginnie Mae)*

Ginnie Mae supports loans insured by the FHA or guaranteed by the VA by guaranteeing pools of mortgages that are packaged for investors.

4.3.3.5 *Federal Home Loan Mortgage Corporation (FHLMC: Freddie Mac)*

Freddie Mac purchases and guarantees mortgage loans and related securities for investment.

4.3.3.6 *Farm Credit System*

The Farm Credit System is a multifaceted federal program created to facilitate farm loans. Various credit institutions provide funds to regional farm credit banks and cooperatives, and these funds are made available as mortgage loans for farms and rural properties.

4.4 Required Lender Disclosures

Lenders who extend credit to consumers for home loans are subject to federal regulations requiring disclosures of detailed information about the credit. The federal Truth in Lending Act, and Regulation Z issued by the Federal Reserve System to implement the act,[1] require several kinds of disclosures.

---

1. 15 U.S.C. §§ 1601–1667f (2006 & Supp. 2010); Truth in Lending (Regulation Z), 12 C.F.R. pt. 226 (2012).

A lender must provide a disclosure before the loan period begins or the first payment is due. The disclosure must show the annual percentage rate, which must take into account the finance charge amounts; the dollar amount to be paid for interest and certain fees; the total amount financed; and the total of payments, which is the loan amount plus fees, finance charges, and interest. Federal and state laws and regulations impose additional requirements on certain kinds of loans, such as high-interest loans, and on all forms of credit when the payment terms change upon certain events. Federal regulations also require lenders to disclose credit terms in a certain way when they advertise.

Federal and state laws also require lenders to provide specific kinds of information to borrowers in connection with the closing costs for mortgage loans. The main source of such requirements is the federal Real Estate Settlement Procedures Act (RESPA),[2] which broadly applies to any federally related residential mortgage loan and any loan involving a federal program that may be sold on the secondary mortgage market.[3] RESPA is intended to provide consumers with "greater and more timely information on the nature and costs of the settlement process" than had been provided by the industry voluntarily and to protect consumers from "unnecessarily high settlement charges caused by certain abusive practices."[4] In general, home loan lenders must give good faith estimates of mortgage loan costs within three business days after receiving a consumer's application for a mortgage loan and before any fees are collected from the consumer, other than a reasonable fee for obtaining a credit history. A good faith estimate has a summary of loan terms and estimated charges, and of key dates, such as when the quoted interest rate expires. Fees that are charged for the loan are known as *origination charges*. The good faith estimate will show eleven categories of charges, including required escrow deposits, services selected by the lender and those that the borrower can select, title work and title insurance, and transfer taxes. The lender must also provide a *Special Information Booklet* that explains the nature of closing costs, the contents of the settlement statement that will be used at closing, the nature of escrow accounts, considerations about the selection of settlement providers, and types of unfair practices and unreasonable charges as to which

---

2. 12 U.S.C. §§ 2601–2617 (2006 & Supp. 2010).
3. *Id.* § 2602.
4. *Id.* § 2601(a).

the borrower should be alert. In general, lenders must wait seven business days after providing these disclosures before closing the loan.

Another important disclosure is the HUD-1 settlement statement provided at closing (described in Section 3.6.1). This important document contains detailed information about the transaction receipts and disbursements, including line items for categories of closing expenses as defined in the regulation instructions.[5]

Federal law also gives borrowers of home loans a right to rescind the transaction by notifying the lender within three business days of the closing of the transaction.

Despite all the information required, lender disclosures can be difficult to fully comprehend, and borrowers who do not understand what the numbers or explanations mean should ask questions and, if necessary, get objective advice from a credit counselor or other professional.

4.5 Mortgage Brokers

Many borrowers use mortgage brokers to find loans. Mortgage brokers provide information about some available loan packages, assist borrowers with completing their loan applications, and help with the gathering of required information, such as credit reports. Often brokers are seen as a central source of information that otherwise may seem bewildering.

Contrary to what some may assume, mortgage brokers are not agents for borrowers. In general, they work as independent contractors. Lenders often provide a discounted wholesale rate for loans that brokers can arrange. The amount charged to the borrower then includes broker compensation. Broker compensation commonly is a percentage or two of the loan amount. Brokers also may receive a set origination fee paid either by the borrower or a lender. They therefore may have a significant financial stake in arranging a particular kind of loan for a borrower.

Mortgage brokers are subject to licensing, education, and bonding requirements administered by the N.C. Commissioner of Banks. The Banking Commission maintains a list of mortgage brokers who are licensed to do business within North Carolina. State statutes impose duties on brokers, including to follow reasonable instructions from the borrower

---

5. Instructions for Completing HUD–1 and HUD–1a Settlement Statements; Sample HUD–1 and HUD–1a Statements, 24 C.F.R. pt. 3500, app. A (2012).

and to keep the borrower informed of "material information that may be expected to influence the borrower's decision and is reasonably accessible to the mortgage broker, including the total compensation the mortgage broker expects to receive from any and all sources in connection with each loan option presented to the borrower."[6] The statutes prohibit many kinds of improper acts, such as misrepresentation of material facts or collection of prohibited fees.[7] Mortgage brokers are subject to disciplinary action for violating their licensing obligations, including the requirement to reimburse borrowers for amounts collected in violation of certain laws.[8]

4.6 Commercial Loans

Although many home lending institutions also make commercial loans, commercial lending is a different business from residential lending. Commercial real estate involves many risks to borrowers and lenders that are not typical with a residential loan. These risks include a more complicated analysis of the real estate's value. Commercial properties are more unique than residential properties, and their value depends at least to some extent on the success of the businesses that operate on them. For example, land on which a shopping center is built can be valuable if the economy is booming and the center is occupied by successful retail merchants, but it can quickly become a troublesome property if the economy turns bad or the tenants do poorly. In addition, commercial and industrial properties are more likely to have problems with such things as zoning limitations or environmental contamination. Commercial loan lenders need to understand how these factors affect the value of real estate and the likelihood of repayment.

Home loans tend to be handled in a routine fashion with standardized documents, but commercial loans typically are made by specialized loan representatives. Commercial banks and other commercial lenders have loan officers who are able to assess businesses and structure complex finance arrangements. Often the point of contact for a business seeking a commercial loan is with a lending representative with whom the business has a prior relationship. Commercial loans also can be obtained through commercial loan brokers.

---

6. Section 53-244.109 of the North Carolina General Statutes (hereinafter G.S.).
7. G.S. 53-244.111.
8. G.S. 53-244.116.

In addition to analysis of the real estate and the business being operated on it, commercial lending involves careful consideration of the borrower's business portfolio and ability to pay. Unlike a residential mortgage loan that usually involves a single borrower or a couple, a commercial borrower often is an entity or association, such as a corporation, limited liability company, or partnership. The ability of these entities and associations to repay loans depends on their business operations and managerial decisions as well as their other business and investment activities.

Business entities such as corporations and limited liability companies have limited liability, which means their creditors are limited to the entities' assets if a lawsuit is necessary for collection of a loan. Consequently, commercial lenders often require financial assurance in addition to a deed of trust. This may include a right to foreclose on other property or assets of the borrower as well as personal guaranties of the main investors in the business. Although large companies with substantial assets may be able to get financing based solely on the assets for which the money will be used, lenders to smaller businesses tend to consider an investor's other assets, including personal properties, as a guaranty (described in the following subsection).

Interest and repayment terms tend to be more complicated for commercial loans than for residential loans. Greater risk means that interest rates tend to be higher than for home loans, and the length of time for repayment may be shorter. Commercial loans commonly have interest rates that are tied to market factors, such as prime lending rates, which fluctuate over time. Commercial loans also sometimes include at least the possibility of an *equity kicker* in what is called an *equity participation* loan. With this kind of arrangement, the lender receives a share of income if it exceeds a certain amount or a share of the sale price if the real estate is sold for more than a certain amount. Usually this involves a lower interest rate than would be required without the participation agreement. These arrangements involve many complex legal and tax considerations.

4.6.1 Guaranties

A *guaranty* is a promise by an individual or an entity to pay a debt for someone else. It is used in real estate finance when the lender is not willing to rely solely on the borrower for repayment. The giver of the guaranty is called the *guarantor*, and the individual or entity for which a debt is being guaranteed is called the *principal*. A guaranty sometimes is called *collateral security.* The most common situation in which a guaranty is given is when the borrower is a company with limited assets, such as a family corporation or limited liability company, and the shareholders or members give a guaranty of payment from their personal assets in case the company does not have sufficient assets to pay off the loan.

A guaranty can be limited to a particular loan or promise, or it can more generally apply to all of the principal's obligations to a lender. It depends on the parties' agreement. A guaranty typically will state that it applies even if the loan or obligations are modified or renewed; this too depends on what the guaranty instrument says. Most guaranty instruments in commercial loan finance are *unconditional* guaranties, meaning that the instrument will state that the guarantor will pay regardless of any defense that the principal borrower may have and without the lender having first to try to collect from the principal. This is also called a *payment* guaranty. A *conditional* guaranty makes the guarantor secondarily responsible. It may provide, for example, that the guarantor will pay only if demand has first been made on the principal borrower and the principal borrower has failed to pay. This is also called a *collection* guaranty.

Just like a promissory note, a guaranty can be unsecured or secured. If it is unsecured, the lender relies on the guarantor's willingness to pay and the possibility of a lawsuit to collect. Or the guarantor can provide security for the guaranty, such as a deed of trust. An example of this kind of an arrangement is when the shareholders of a family corporation give a personal guarantee of the corporation's loan and provide a deed of trust on their home as security for that guaranty. Guarantors need to understand that providing a guaranty puts their homes and personal wealth at risk.

4.7 Construction Loans

Approvals for construction loans involve many of the same considerations as approvals for commercial loans. The lender will consider the value of the land being used as security and the anticipated value of the completed construction. This is straightforward if the construction is a single home, but the calculation is more complex when the loan is for a multiunit development, commercial real estate, or industrial site. The lender will review the engineering and architectural designs as well as information about the ability of the site to support the construction, such as environmental and soil tests. They also will consider the quality of the proposed construction and likely will insist on the right to approve the contractor who will be doing the work. These lenders want to ensure that the contractor has a reputation for high-quality work as well as reliability for completing work in a timely manner and on budget. In sum, with a construction loan the lender is relying on others' sound decisions and performance. The loan will be subject to special considerations in the way it is structured and managed.

4.7.1 Loan Structure

Construction loans usually are structured in one of two ways. Under the simplest approach, a single construction loan is made with a large installment paid at the beginning to enable the borrower to purchase land and then periodic additional payments to be made during construction as costs are incurred. The borrower will be charged a fee at the beginning of the loan and additional fees for loan management. The term of a construction loan is likely to be short: typically a year or two. The interest rates tend to be variable and higher than loans for completed construction, which reflects the greater risk to the lender. Lenders will monitor construction and payments to contractors and subcontractors to ensure that the project value exceeds the amount loaned to date. Under this simple approach, the borrower will obtain a *permanent* loan from a lender to pay the construction loan when it becomes due. That permanent loan will be long-term, and the principal and interest are paid just as with any other mortgage loan.

The second common method for construction financing is for a lender to offer a combination loan in which the original construction loan is replaced with a second loan from the same lender. The advantage of this arrangement is that the borrower is assured of the permanent loan, and the charges for the construction loan may at least in part be applied to the charges for the permanent loan. A disadvantage to the borrower is being locked into an arrangement with the same lender and not having the option of shopping for a more favorable arrangement that may be available when the permanent loan is needed.

4.7.2 Construction Loan Management

Owners sometimes finance construction projects in a manner similar to loans for existing construction, that is, by agreeing to pay a builder a fixed price for the real estate that is paid in large part through a loan. Essentially the builder is both the seller and the lender. In real estate financing the term *construction loan* generally means a three-party arrangement in which a loan is being extended by a lender to a borrower for construction to be completed by a third-party builder. This arrangement involves considerations that are not involved with existing construction.

One of the challenges of a construction loan is the unpredictability of construction costs and the value of the completed project. Lenders can assess the value of an existing home based on market information about comparable properties. A construction loan is based on a prediction about what the future value of the completed project is expected to be. The amount of the loan for construction includes both *hard* costs for labor and materials and *soft* costs for such things as design and testing, project administration, permits, real estate taxes, and insurance premiums. All of these amounts are subject to change as the project goes along, and construction costs can greatly exceed initial expectations.

Construction lending is made even more complex because the approved total loan amount is based on the value of a completed project, but money must be loaned during construction well before that value is created. The lender therefore disburses the loan in draws, or installments, hoping that the value of the project and the lender's security increases on pace with the total outstanding loan amount. Typically the lender will disburse a construction loan in draws based on documentation the borrower submits of actual labor and materials provided. This will be either the full amount of actual costs incurred or a substantial percentage with a retained amount withheld until the project is completed as additional protection to the lender. The lender's construction manager reviews the documentation throughout construction and inspects the work and makes disbursements only as phases progress according to plan.

4.7.3 Construction Liens

Construction mortgages introduce yet another complication because those who are doing the work and providing the materials look to the value they contribute to the real estate as security for their payments. Lawmakers have long given construction laborers and material providers a right in the real estate they improve as protection for payment. Complicated laws govern how these rights are reconciled among each other and with respect to the construction lender. In general the statutes attempt to protect labor and material providers' rights to payment while still enabling owners to get the necessary funds for the project work from lenders.

North Carolina gives those who perform work or provide materials, or provide professional design or surveying services, a right to a *mechanic's lien* in their work to secure payment. To claim this lien, the person who is owed money files an action with the superior court clerk "not later than 120 days after the last furnishing of labor or materials at the site of the improvement by the person claiming the lien."[9] The claimant can then bring an action in superior court to enforce the lien no "later than 180 days after the last furnishing of labor or materials at the site of the improvement by the person claiming the claim of lien on real property."[10] If the party's claim is approved, the court can order property to be sold to pay the judgment.[11] In reality the threat of the lien means that developers and lenders are careful about keeping contractors, subcontractors, and materials providers current in their payments.

The relative rights of various claimants depend on with whom the provider dealt in the construction process. Someone who has a direct contract with the owner, usually called a *contractor*, has a lien on the owner's real estate for the full amount owed under the contract.[12] Others have a more limited lien. A subcontractor is someone who deals with the contractor on the owner's project. A subcontractor is entitled to a lien on the amount the owner owes the contractor, and someone who provided labor or materials to a subcontractor has a lien limited to what is owed to that subcontractor and a secondary right to claim what is owed by the owner to the contractor.[13] The order of priorities for more remote subcontractors is similar.

In general, a construction lender will have priority lien for all loan amounts used in the construction if certain conditions are met, including a disclosure in the deed of trust of the maximum amount of secured obligations and the period during which they are to be incurred.[14] What makes labor and materials liens such a worrisome thing for construction lenders is that their priority relates to when the labor or materials were first provided, which can be well before a something is filed with a court giving notice of the lien.[15] This means that a labor or materials provider could have a right to collection from the owner that is prior to the rights

---

9. G.S. 44A-10 through -12.
10. G.S. 44A-13.
11. G.S. 44A-14(b).
12. G.S. 44A-8.
13. G.S. 44A-18(1), (2).
14. G.S. 45-68.
15. G.S. 44A-10(1b).

in a deed of trust recorded without any notice of a labor and materials lien. Consequently, before making loans, lenders may require owners to provide information about whether there has been any recent work at the real estate.

The rules regarding competing priorities among purchase money and construction lenders, and providers of labor and materials, depend on the particular circumstances and a number of complex statutes, and it is sometimes necessary to work through a number of difficult issues before those priorities can be clearly seen. When projects greatly exceed projected cost, or labor or materials providers fail to perform as promised, sorting out the various claims can be complicated and contentious. Careful construction lenders therefore tend to be very vigilant about the progress of the work and the status of payments.

4.7.4 Letters of Credit and Performance Bonds

A *letter of credit* is a type of financing arrangement commonly encountered in real estate development that provides a form of guaranty of performance. A *standby letter of credit* is issued by a bank to guarantee a payment or performance by the applicant. The bank agrees to pay a third party if the conditions described in the letter of credit occur as shown on a notice of claim and supporting documentation. The bank does not investigate the merits of the claim; it pays the amount and then looks to the applicant to recover what is paid. The cost for a letter of credit typically is a few percent of the amount of the credit, depending on the market, the applicant, the security that the applicant provides, and the purpose.

Letters of credit are commonly used with developments involving roads. When approving the project the local government wants assurances that the roads will be completed as planned and not left as a problem for the lot owners and local government. The local government may require a letter of credit for the cost of road completion. If the roads are not completed, the local government can make a claim on the letter of credit and use the payment to complete the roads.

A *performance bond* is a guarantee issued by a surety, such as an insurance company, to pay for the costs of completion if the party whose performance is assured does not perform. With a bond the insurer will confirm that a claim made on it meets certain conditions, but the insurer does not become involved in a dispute between the person making the claim and the party whose performance is assured. Typical costs for performance bonds are a few percent of the bond amount.

4.8 Reverse Mortgages

Many people are able to pay off their mortgage loans during their lives, leaving them with real estate that has equity in the full amount of its market value. Substantial equity can result also from large increases in value of the real estate. Equity in real estate is an asset, but it is not a *liquid* asset that can be used to pay bills. An owner can tap into this equity with a financing technique known as a *reverse mortgage*. It is called reverse because the owner receives from rather than makes payments to an institutional lender in exchange for a deed of trust or mortgage. With a reverse mortgage, a lender agrees to provide money in installments during the owner's life, and the owner agrees that the loan will be repaid, with interest, at a certain date, when the owner dies or sells the real estate, or when the owner stops using it for a residence. Generally there is no tax on the payments made to the owner. Reverse mortgages are most commonly used by seniors who have paid off their mortgages and want to use the value in their homes to get regular payments that can be used for expenses.

The balance of a loan subject to a reverse mortgage goes up rather than down. The amount that a lender is willing to loan is based on the lender's estimate of the equity in the real estate considering what someone would pay for it on the condition that it will not be available until after the owner's death. Someone naturally will pay less for real estate with this delay, so a lender will loan less for a reverse mortgage than for a standard mortgage.

When the owner of real estate subject to a reverse mortgage dies, the real estate is sold and the proceeds are applied to pay the loan. Someone who wants to inherit the real estate would have to get a different loan to pay off the reverse mortgage. Prior to death the owner has an option of eliminating the reverse mortgage by repaying the entire amount owed or by refinancing. Reverse mortgages usually require borrowers to repay the loan if they no longer use their homes as their residence or if they default on other obligations. These other obligations include such things as paying the real estate taxes and utilities and keeping the real estate insured.

There are several typical plans for drawing payments in a reverse mortgage arrangement. With the *tenure* plan, the borrower receives equal monthly payments for life as long as the real estate is the borrower's principal residence. With a *term* plan, the payments last for a number of years. With a *line of credit* (see Section 4.2), the borrower receives installments as requested, up to a maximum amount. Combinations of these plans also are available.

Owners want to be careful not to get a reverse mortgage that could force them to sell their home if they live longer than they expect. The reverse mortgage can guarantee that owners may keep their home as long as they live without having to repay the loan provided they meet the mortgage conditions. The FHA's Home Equity Conversion Mortgage Program (HECM) has requirements that are intended to ensure that reverse mortgages are reasonable and consistent with their intended purpose.

4.9 Deeds of Trust and Other Security Instruments

Most privately owned real estate in North Carolina is the subject of a deed of trust that the owner has given to a lender as security for repayment of money loaned to purchase the real estate. The laws governing deeds of trust are complex, and the details change over time as a result of federal and state legislation. For example, the federal Servicemembers Civil Relief Act (SCRA) recently provided members of the military service with a number of benefits and protections for themselves and their families, including interest rate limitations, protection against eviction, and a right for servicemembers who are unable to appear in a court proceeding to a postponement for at least ninety days.[16] State law provisions complement the federal law and prohibit a foreclosure hearing to proceed during a debtor's military service or within ninety days after, unless the servicemember agrees to proceed during that time. No lender may proceed with a hearing on a foreclosure without first filing a certification with the clerk of court that the hearing does not violate this prohibition.[17] This is only one example of recent changes in the law governing deeds of trust. Anyone with a question about how current law affects their rights or obligations should consult a lawyer who is familiar with current laws and practices as they may apply to the particular circumstances involved.

4.9.1 Parties to Deeds of Trust and Mortgages

The vast majority of real estate sales are made possible by substantial loans from mortgage lenders. Lenders take the financial risk because they get rights to sell the real estate if their loans are not repaid. In legal terms, the property is said to function as *security* for the loan, and the instrument used

---

16. 50 U.S.C. app. § 501 through § 506 (2006 & Supp. 2010).
17. G.S. 45-21.12A.

to create this arrangement is called a *security instrument*. Most people think of this arrangement as a *mortgage*, which is a common form of security interest in real estate in which the owner is the *mortgagor* and the lender is the *mortgagee*. With a mortgage, the mortgagor gives the mortgagee a right to foreclose if the loan goes into default, and the mortgagee agrees to release the mortgage after full payment has been made.

In North Carolina, the most commonly used legal instrument for a mortgage loan is a *deed of trust*. It is functionally the same as a mortgage but uses a different legal framework. With a deed of trust, the owner gives a deed transferring the legal title to the real estate to a *trustee*, who often is a lawyer or other individual compensated for this role. The trustee holds the title only as security for the loan and is bound to re-convey the real estate to the owner after the loan has been repaid. Even though the deed of trust or mortgage involves what is technically a conveyance by deed of the real estate to a trustee or mortgagee, for most purposes the law treats the owner as having all rights of ownership except as limited by the deed of trust or mortgage.

With both deeds of trust and mortgages, the right to foreclose is a *power of sale*. If the loan is not paid when due or there is another default under the loan or security instrument, the real estate can be sold to satisfy the debt according to procedures set by statute. This is called a *foreclosure* because the sale forecloses or cuts off the owner's right to get the real estate back free of the deed of trust or mortgage.

4.9.2 Deed of Trust Priorities

A typical deed of trust involves two primary legal documents that define the owner's and lender's obligations and rights. A *promissory note* specifies the amount and payment schedule for the loan. A deed of trust will incorporate this payment agreement.

North Carolina's real estate recording laws give lenders a way to tell anyone who might be interested in the real estate about the existence of a deed of trust and right to foreclose. A lender who first records a deed of trust will have priority over later-recorded deeds of trust and other security interests. Everyone who makes a loan after the recording is deemed to be aware of that prior deed of trust regardless of whether they actually searched the records of the register of deeds. Usually a lender who records a deed of trust on real estate when another deed of trust is already on record does so knowingly, becoming a second priority. Rarely these priorities are switched by lender agreement with a *subordination agreement* executed by the lender of the subordinated deed of trust, in which a first-recorded interest is by agreement made subordinate to a second-recorded interest. Very few unrecorded creditor rights take priority over a deed of trust. The most common exception is a tax lien.

Priorities become important in a foreclosure context when funds are insufficient to pay off all of the secured debt. Deeds of trust and other liens are paid in the order of their priority of right. Consider the following example: real estate is sold at foreclosure for $250,000 by a lender with a first-priority deed of trust who is owed $200,000 and incurs $2,500 in foreclosure expenses; the real estate is also subject to a second deed of trust on which $15,000 is owed; in addition, there is a tax lien for $5,000. The disbursements of the foreclosure sale proceeds would be as follows:

Tax lien	$ 5,000
First lender	202,500
Second lender	15,000
Owner	27,500
Total	$ 250,000

In this scenario all creditors receive payment and the owner gets the balance. Assume instead that the real estate had declined in value so that only $200,000 could be raised at foreclosure. The second lender and owner would receive nothing, as shown here:

Tax lien	$ 5,000
First lender	195,000
Second lender	0
Owner	0
Total	$ 200,000

Sometimes a deed of trust involves an ongoing arrangement in which the owner receives one amount from the lender initially and additional funds later. The later disbursements are called *future advances* and may be included in the total sum that is subject to the already recorded deed of trust. A recorded deed of trust secures future advances if it clearly says that they will be covered and the deed of trust identifies both the maximum principal amount to be secured and the time period during which they may be extended.[18]

A deed of trust will contain many promises regarding rights in the real estate, such as to pay taxes, maintain the real estate in good condition, and

---

18. G.S. 45-68.

keep it insured. Although most transactions involve a single note and a single deed of trust, the financing arrangement can be more complicated. For example, a deed of trust can apply to more than one note, to a line of credit in which the amount of the loan may be increased with disbursements over time, or to a personal guaranty of someone else's obligations to the lender. The security arrangement also can be more complicated than a single deed of trust, as is often the case with loans made to commercial enterprises. For example, there can be other types of security instruments, such as an assignment of leases and rents (see Section 4.1) by which the owner agrees that the lender can directly collect rental income upon a default in payment of the loan. Commercial real estate transactions often involve complex and interrelated security instruments and underlying promissory notes.

A deed of trust will only give the lender rights to the real estate that are described in the instrument. The real estate description need not exactly match the owner's deed, but it usually does to avoid giving the impression that something else is intended. The deed of trust will be effective if the real estate intended to be mortgaged can be ascertained. To the surprise of most people who read a deed of trust for the first time, the buildings will not be specifically described and may not even be mentioned. Buildings are automatically included as real estate when they are permanently constructed on the land, and unless there is a clear agreement otherwise conveyance of an interest in the land includes the buildings. Buildings that are constructed off-site and placed on a foundation on the land, such as mobile and manufactured homes, are treated the same as buildings constructed directly on the land. Mobile manufactured housing becomes real estate subject to a mortgage when placed on a site and tied into required utilities. A lender may also obtain a security interest in manufactured housing before it is part of the real estate, with priority over a deed of trust on the land on which it is installed, by complying with the Uniform Commercial Code (UCC).[19] A manufactured home that is registered with the Division of Motor Vehicles can become part of the real estate on which it is situated if the home is on land of the homeowner or on land for which the homeowner has a lease of at least twenty years and the title is surrendered and a required form of affidavit is recorded with the register of deeds.[20]

---

19. G.S. 25-9-334; G.S. 9-311(a)(2).
20. G.S. 20-109.2; G.S. 47-20.6.

Fixtures involve special considerations. A fixture is something that begins as non–real estate property but becomes a permanent part of real estate, such as installed lighting or a built-in appliance. An item becomes part of the real estate and subject to a deed of trust when it is permanently attached, unless the parties agree to treat it otherwise. Security interests in fixtures can be obtained by recording a UCC financing statement at the office of the register of deeds or by recording a deed of trust that contains statutorily required information.[21] Lenders usually record in both the personal property filing offices and the register of deeds to ensure that they have an enforceable interest.

4.9.3 Owners' Promises

Most deeds of trust follow standard forms, especially for home loans. The typical form contains two main types of components: a power of sale and mortgage covenants.

Deeds of trust grant a power of sale to the trustee, who can sell the real estate for the lender if there is a default in the terms of the note or deed of trust. This language allows the lender to follow a process specified in the North Carolina statutes for foreclosure over which the superior courts have jurisdiction. The right to foreclose is triggered upon a *default*, which includes the borrower's failure to make note payments when they are due or to violate other promises made in the deed of trust, such as paying the real estate taxes or keeping the real estate insured. These promises are called *mortgage covenants*. Before agreeing to a deed of trust the borrower should carefully read the entire document to understand all the covenants that can result in triggering the right of foreclosure. The courts generally will enforce the terms of a deed of trust *as they are written*.

Deeds of trust for home loans typically are prepared on pre-printed forms containing standard language to comply with state and federal law and enable lenders to transfer the loans and deeds of trust to other lenders or investors. The typical deed of trust form contains the following legal phraseology:

> Borrower covenants that borrower is lawfully seised of estate hereby conveyed and has the right to grant and convey the Property and that the Property is unencumbered, except for encumbrances of record. Borrower warrants and will defend generally the title to the Property

---

21. G.S. 25-9-502(c).

against all claims and demands, subject to any encumbrances of record.

This language is likely unintelligible to someone unfamiliar with real estate law. Obviously the words *seised* and *encumbrance* are not used in everyday language, yet they express the core of what the owner is agreeing to do. Although the words may seem mystifying, the nature of the promises they embody is not so hard to understand. This is why borrowers should ask as many questions as necessary to fully understand the various details of an agreement.

When owners sign a deed of trust that says they are "lawfully seised of estate hereby conveyed," they are confirming that the real estate is rightfully theirs and that they have the legal power to give the deed of trust to the lender. This confirms an obvious expectation: if the person giving the deed of trust did not really own the real estate it describes, the lender can sue the person for breach of this covenant and seek damages for recoupment of the loan and other expenses.

When the owner promises to "warrant" and "defend" the title, the owner is promising that if someone else makes a claim to the real estate described in the deed of trust, the owner will take legal action to defend against the claim. This protects the lender's reliance on the value of the real estate as security for the loan.

Typical deeds of trust contain a number of other owner promises. For example, the owner promises to pay the real estate taxes before authorities can acquire rights to take action against the real estate. This is important to the lender because a government unit that is owed real estate taxes has a priority right to sell the real estate to pay the taxes, which puts the lender's security in the real estate at risk. As further protection, lenders commonly require owners to make regular deposits in an escrow account from which periodic tax payments can be made when they are due rather than rely on the owners to have sufficient funds to make the payments in a lump sum before the deadline. Deeds of trust also will contain a promise by the borrower not to allow any other deeds of trust on the real estate that could take priority without the lender's agreement.

Deeds of trust also commonly require the borrower to get insurance for the property against fire and other hazards with an *extended coverage* policy that has deductibles acceptable to the lender. The lender requires this insurance to protect the value of the structures and may require that the premiums be paid out of an escrow account similar to what is used for local government real estate taxes. The deed of trust probably gives the lender the right to approve the insurance company, provided this decision is made reasonably. The deed of trust likely will give the lender the right to obtain coverage directly from an insurance company if the owner fails to do so or a policy expires and to add the premiums for such policies to the secured indebtedness owed by the borrower. The deed of trust also likely will provide that the lender must be notified if a loss occurs for which a payment under the insurance policy will be made. Most deeds of trust specify that the insurance proceeds are first applied to restore the buildings, unless to do so is not economically feasible or the lender's security would be diminished, in which case the lender can insist that the proceeds be applied to the loan.

A deed of trust on a home will contain a number of provisions required by federal or state law. For example, it may give the borrower, under federal law, the right to reinstate the loan and deed of trust after a default and before foreclosure, such as within five days before a foreclosure sale. The borrower likely will have additional rights under state law, such as the right to reinstate the loan at any time prior to the foreclosure sale or expiration of the deadline for an upset bid by paying the obligation and the lender's foreclosure expenses.

4.10 Servicers and Assignments

Rarely are mortgage loans held and managed throughout their existence by the originating lenders. The promissory note signed by the homeowner is very likely to be negotiable, meaning that the lender may transfer it at any time and that that assignee may further assign it. The deed of trust that accompanies the note is likely to provide that it too is transferrable without the homeowner's approval or, even, knowledge.

Mortgage loan transferability is an essential part of the lending markets. Most lenders who are in the business of originating mortgage loans make their profit with the fees they charge at closing, not by keeping the loans until they are repaid. Lenders often trade the mortgage loans they originate, and the right to collect repayment, in exchange for a share of a large pool of mortgages. They sell the loans in what is called the *secondary mortgage market*. This market was first established by federal agencies to pool resources and spread the risk of default, which made financing for homeownership more widely available to more people. Most secondary mortgage pools are organized by the federal agencies described in Section 4.3.3, the biggest being the Federal National Mortgage Association (FNMA). Commonly referred to as Fannie Mae, FNMA is the largest investor in the U.S. residential mortgage market.

Loans are often *securitized.* In the secondary market arrangement, trustees collect mortgage loans and put them into pools, with shares sold to investors. These pools lessen the risk of investment because generally the number of loans being repaid far outweighs the impact of the few that are not. The serious economic difficulties that began in 2008 were in large part the result of lending practices through which far too many loans were issued and securitized for borrowers who did not have the means to repay them. Also, many lending decisions were based on highly inflated estimates of the value of the real estate serving as collateral. As the percentage of nonperforming loans dramatically increased, the pools were no longer profitable, and many of the participants experienced disastrous financial difficulties.

Most borrowers are not affected by the transfer of their loans into the secondary market or into a securitization pool. Borrowers do not have to keep track of the ownership status of their loans. They make their payments to a *servicer* regardless of what institution or investment group holds the loan at any given time. Once the loan is paid off, either according to the original schedule or earlier as a result of a sale or a refinancing, the funds will be transferred through the servicers, who will handle the required paperwork to show satisfaction of the loan at the office of the register of deeds. When loans are not paid when due, the servicer becomes the contact for negotiating a restructuring of the loan, and if foreclosure proceedings are initiated they will be in the name of the current holder of the loan.

Many loans are managed through Mortgage Electronic Registration Systems, Inc., commonly known as MERS. In 1997, major institutions in the mortgage industry, including Freddie Mac and Ginnie Mae, created MERS to reduce the costs of transferring mortgage loans. Rather than record an assignment every time a mortgage was transferred, the initial lender would assign the loan to MERS as a *nominee.* Transfers of ownership are then recorded with MERS. MERS became the holder of record of a majority of residential loans in the United States. Legal disputes arose when many of the loans became the subject of foreclosure and the record of who actually held the loan and was thereby entitled to conduct the foreclosure was called into question. This caused some courts to halt foreclosure proceedings. Some borrowers reported that their financial troubles were caused or exacerbated by their inability to deal with someone who had the interest and authority to correct a record keeping error with the mortgage or to stop a foreclosure for other good reasons.

In recent years, many borrowers have had problems communicating with loan servicers. This has been especially troublesome in situations where loan payments appear to have been misapplied and the borrower gets a notice of default but is unable to reach someone who can correct the record. Federal consumer protection laws attempt to handle such problems. The Real Estate Settlement Procedures Act (RESPA) requires loan servicers to notify borrowers in writing of any assignment of a mortgage loan within fifteen days of the assignment's effective date.[22] As long as the borrower makes a timely payment to the old servicer within sixty days of the loan transfer, the borrower cannot be penalized. The notice must include the name and address of the new servicer, toll-free telephone numbers, and the date the new servicer will begin accepting payments. The Truth in Lending Act[23] requires an assignee to notify the borrower in writing within thirty days after a loan is transferred. The notice must include the assignee's identity, address and phone number, the date of transfer, the contact information for an agent or party having authority to act on behalf of the assignee, and the location of the place where transfer of ownership of the debt is recorded. Servicers and assignees that violate these requirements are subject to liability for damages, penalties, costs, and lawyers' fees.[24]

4.11 Records of Satisfaction

The loan relationship that is a subject of the deed of trust terminates when the loan is paid. But the deed of trust continues to affect the owner's interest in the real estate until a document called a *satisfaction* is recorded. The absence of a public record indicating that a deed of trust has been satisfied does not necessarily mean that an unpaid loan obligation exists or that there is an enforceable lien on the real estate. Nevertheless, a recorded deed of

---

22. 12 U.S.C.A. § 2605 (Supp. 2011); Mortgage Servicing Transfers, 24 C.F.R. § 3500.21(d) (2012).

23. 15 U.S.C.A. § 1641(g)(1) (Supp. 2011).

24. 12 U.S.C.A. § 2605(f) (Supp. 2011); 15 U.S.C.A. § 1640(a) (Supp. 2011).

trust continues to be an apparent encumbrance on the real estate, thereby impairing the real estate's marketability, until an instrument showing that the deed of trust has been satisfied is recorded.

Ordinarily the secured party lender attends to making a record of satisfaction by generating a routine document for recording that can be processed without special attention. A *satisfaction of security instrument* or *trustee's satisfaction of a deed of trust* identifies the original parties and the original instrument's recording information. A satisfaction of security instrument must be signed by the secured creditor, and a trustee's satisfaction of a deed must be signed by a trustee or substitute trustee, and both instruments must be acknowledged.[25] Lenders also may use a similar *notice of satisfaction* form, and owners of notes and secured creditors may use a *certificate of satisfaction* form.[26] The North Carolina General Statutes require such documents to identify the deed of trust or other security instrument that has been satisfied, its recording data, the parties to it, and the office in which it was recorded, and allow for the use of a variety of similar forms. "No particular phrasing is required for a satisfaction of a security instrument" or for a trustee's satisfaction, and the statutes provide forms that include the minimum information needed to deem the record sufficient.[27] There is no fee for recording a notice of satisfaction. Recording fees for deeds of trust are higher than for other instruments, which reflects an effective pre-payment of the cost of recording a satisfaction when the mortgage loan is paid off.

State law also still allows a mortgagee or trustee to make a record of satisfaction with a *quitclaim deed* (see Section 3.5.1.3) or *release deed* or other conveyance instrument signed, acknowledged, and recorded.[28] To be recorded, this type of document must be acknowledged in the same manner as a deed and is subject to the same recording requirements. In North Carolina, deeds of release are the most common method for releasing a deed of trust from a portion of the covered real estate, for example when a deed of trust applies to a large parcel from which several lots are developed and the lender is releasing only one lot in connection with a partial payment of the obligation secured by the deed of trust.

---

25. G.S. 45-36.10, .11, .20, .21.
26. G.S. 47-46.1; G.S. 47-46.2.
27. G.S. 45-36.11, .21.
28. G.S. 45-41.

By North Carolina statute, a lender must submit a satisfaction for recording within thirty days after the loan has been paid in full.[29] The lender is liable for any actual damages caused by a failure to comply. After this deadline has passed, and if a lender still fails to get a satisfaction recorded within another thirty days after receiving a request by the borrower by certified mail, the lender is liable for $1,000, reasonable lawyers' fees, and court costs.[30] As described in the following subsection, North Carolina has a procedure for a lawyer to record a document known as an affidavit of satisfaction that has the effect of a satisfaction when there is proof that the loan has been paid but a satisfaction instrument cannot be obtained from a lender.

A method of satisfaction that was in common use for many years was *satisfaction upon presentation*. Several approaches were used, but the most common was for the lender or the lender's lawyer to present to the register of deeds both the original note and the original deed of trust, each endorsed as paid by the lender. The register then made a record of satisfaction consisting of portions of the original instruments that identified the deed of trust and the original parties to it, its recording data, and the endorsements of payment. In recent years, fewer and fewer satisfactions were being recorded in this manner, and also to address problems dealing with original instruments, the General Assembly ended the use of satisfaction upon presentation effective October 1, 2011.

4.11.1 Affidavits of Satisfaction

If a lender fails to provide a satisfaction as required, a lawyer licensed to practice law in North Carolina, acting as *satisfaction agent*, may give notice to the secured creditor of intent to record an *affidavit of satisfaction*.[31] The borrower's lawyer's notice of satisfaction must contain information prescribed by statute about the instrument and about having completed the procedure for demanding a satisfaction instrument from the secured creditor, and it must be signed by the borrower's lawyer as satisfaction agent and be acknowledged.[32]

---

29. G.S. 45-36.9(a).
30. G.S. 45-36.9(c).
31. G.S. 45-36.15.
32. G.S. 45-36.16.

4.12 Foreclosure

Deeds of trust typically contain an *acceleration clause* that causes the full amount of a loan to be due when there has been any default. The most common type of default is a failure to make a payment by the due date and any applicable grace period. The right to foreclose and sell real estate is essential to a lender's willingness to make the substantial loans needed for real estate purchase and ownership.

The mortgage lending industry depends on collecting payments from performing loans, not on foreclosing and owning properties. Reasonable lenders will not immediately commence foreclosure when a payment is missed. They will abide for a few months before beginning the foreclosure process, discussing alternatives with the borrower. One possibility is loan modification, which can involve changing the payments to enable the borrower to catch up. This is a good possibility when the real estate is worth much more than the loan, because the lender continues to expect to be able to recover the full amount of the loan if foreclosure later becomes necessary. The lender also may be willing to wait a while to give the borrower a chance to sell the real estate and pay off the loan from the proceeds. Even unreasonable lenders know that an agreement for less than full recovery may be better than foreclosure, taking into account expenses and delays, the uncertainties of foreclosure sale prices, and the courts' wariness of uncompromising attitudes toward homeowners in financial difficulty.

Both the lender and borrower have few options if the value of the home drops below the amount owed on the loan, which can occur if there has been a decline in market values, especially if the amount of the initial loan was already close to the real estate's full value. Borrowers in this situation often feel trapped because the real estate cannot be sold for a price high enough to pay off the loan and remove the deed of trust from the real estate so that it can be sold. Lenders sometimes consider a *short sale* of a home subject to a deed of trust, agreeing to release the deed of trust and allow a sale and accept something less than full payment. Another approach is a *deed in lieu of foreclosure*, in which the lender agrees to take back the real estate in exchange for not pursuing foreclosure. Each lender has its own approach to determining how best to resolve a troubled loan.

Lenders propose or agree to alternatives to foreclosure when they can see that doing so will result in a better outcome for them. Borrowers need to look at the possibilities from their own perspectives. One factor sometimes overlooked is the tax consequences of a forgiveness of debt. In general, the forgiveness of debt is considered income to the borrower, and a borrower who recently was unable to pay a loan may not expect a tax liability or have the resources to pay it. In some circumstances involving home loans, the tax laws allow borrowers not to treat such a release of debt as income. Current tax law would need to be checked carefully and seeking legal advice may be appropriate.

Many of these alternatives depend on the history of the loan and the lender's and borrower's cooperation. The following subsection describes the process that lenders follow when they proceed with foreclosure.

4.12.1 Foreclosure by Statutory Power of Sale

The source of a lender's right to foreclose by power of sale is contained in the deed of trust that the borrower signed. In other words, the lender is enforcing a promise that the borrower made, and the lender must comply with the terms and conditions that are stated in the deed of trust. As noted above, lenders tend to use standard forms for deeds of trust for home loans, so the process tends to be the very similar for all lenders. Commercial mortgage lending often involves complex arrangements and specially negotiated terms and conditions, but the basic right to foreclose according to the statutory procedure is the same.

Obviously a foreclosure has severe consequences for the owner, which in a home loan context could include loss of the home. The process is subject to court oversight, and a borrower has the opportunity to stop the foreclosure by showing the court that the lender does not in fact have the right to foreclosure according to the loan documents or that there is some other violation of the law. In addition, by statute, throughout the process the borrower may stop the foreclosure by paying the amount owed and the expenses of the sale incurred to date.[33] Usually foreclosure continues without such court intervention. Under normal circumstances it takes about three or four months from start to the conclusion of the sale.

To start foreclosure, the lender notifies the borrower that a default has been noted and the loan is being accelerated and due in full. The lender begins the court process by filing a notice of a hearing with the clerk of superior court.[34] A notice of sale must be posted in an area designated by the clerk, at least twenty days before the sale. The notice also must appear once a week for at least two successive weeks in a newspaper published and qualified for legal advertising in the county in which the real estate is situ-

---

33. G.S. 45-21.20.
34. G.S. 45-21.16.

ated, with the first publication at least seven days before the last publication and the last publication no more than ten days before the sale.[35] The notice must contain information specified by statute, including a reference to the deed of trust; the hour and place of sale; a description of the real estate to be sold; the terms of the sale, including any deposit requirements; mention that the real estate will be sold subject to taxes; and a statement about whether the real estate is being sold subject to other liens or rights as well as any other information specifically required by the deed of trust. Additional requirements may apply to notices of foreclosure on buildings in which there are residential tenants.[36] Notice must be mailed by first-class mail to each party entitled to notice at least twenty days before the sale.[37] Those who are entitled to receive notice of the upcoming sale obviously include the owner but also anyone else who has filed a *request for notice* with the register of deeds, as would likely be the case with other lenders who have made home equity loans after the foreclosing lender's deed of trust was recorded.[38]

The clerk of court will check to confirm a valid debt owed to the foreclosing lender, the existence of a default, and compliance with the notice requirements.[39] Statutes may require the clerk to examine certain other circumstances, such as whether extended time periods or notice requirements apply to the particular kind of loan that is the subject of the foreclosure.[40]

If the real estate that is the subject of the foreclosure is occupied by the owner, the statutes require that the clerk ask at the hearing about the lender's efforts to resolve the default, unless an affidavit of those efforts has been submitted. The clerk may postpone action for not more than sixty days if "the clerk finds that there is good cause to believe that additional time or additional measures have a reasonable likelihood of resolving the delinquency without foreclosure," based on such factors as the communications that have occurred, the debtor's intent and ability to make payments, the lender's offers to modify the loan, and evidence of good faith. A further extension can be made after another hearing.[41]

---

35. G.S. 45-21.17.
36. G.S. 45-21.16A.
37. G.S. 21.17(4).
38. G.S. 21.17A.
39. G.S. 45-21.16(d).
40. G.S. 45-21.16(c).
41. G.S. 45-21.16C.

State law restricts foreclosures on real estate owned by those who are in military service. Lenders may not exercise the power of sale during or within ninety days after active duty military service or a call to federal active service for more than thirty days. This right can be waived in writing during service in a separate instrument,[42] which may occur if the service member does not wish to contest the foreclosure as part of an agreement with the lender.

The typical foreclosure sale is an auction at which competing bids are made in increasing amounts until the bidding stops. The foreclosing lender will likely participate to protect its interest by bidding and purchasing for later resale at an amount higher than bids that are substantially lower than market value. The foreclosing lender must file a preliminary report with the clerk within five days of the sale, with prescribed information about the sale and the price.[43]

Within ten days after a foreclosure sale, anyone can purchase the real estate with an *upset bid* that is higher than the foreclosure price. By statute, the upset price must be at least five percent more than the sale price and cannot be less than $750 more than the sale price. The bidder must make a deposit of at least five percent plus any other bond or other security that the clerk orders to be posted.[44] A qualifying upset bid triggers another opportunity for others to upset that price by bidding a greater price within ten days.

Federal or state law may also provide tenants with rights when their residence is in real estate subject to foreclosure. For example, federal law may provide tenants in a building on which a foreclosure is being conducted a minimum time before an eviction can proceed.

4.12.2 Foreclosure by Action

As noted above, almost all foreclosures follow the statutory power of sale procedure based on an agreement in the deed of trust. The statutes provide an alternative method for a lender to conduct a *foreclosure by action*. With this method, the lender brings an action in either the district court or superior court in the county in which the land is situated. The lender asks the court for a decree ordering the real estate to be sold to pay off the loan,

---

42. G.S. 45-21.12A.
43. G.S. 45-21.26.
44. G.S. 45-21.27.

and either the trustee or someone else will be appointed as a commissioner to conduct the sale and convey the real estate.[45]

4.12.3 Liability for Unpaid Balance

In most cases, a lender has the right to sue a borrower for the balance owed on a note if the foreclosure sale does not bring in enough money to completely pay off the loan and reimburse the lender for foreclosure expenses. For example, if the borrower owed $200,000, and the real estate was sold for a fair market price of only $150,000, the lender may bring a lawsuit against the borrower to recover the remaining $50,000 out of the borrower's other assets or on a payment schedule. If such a collection action is brought after the creditor purchased the real estate itself at the foreclosure, the borrower may defeat or offset the claim by proving that the value of the real estate sold was fairly equal to the amount of the secured debt or that the amount bid was substantially less than the real estate's true value.[46] This is unlikely to be the case.

The law is different when the loan for the purchase price was made by the seller rather than a third-party lender. A law known as the *anti-deficiency statute* prohibits a seller who made a loan for the purchase of real estate from suing the owner for what is still owed on the secured note after the deed of trust is foreclosed.[47] In addition, the North Carolina General Statutes bar deficiency judgments for certain kinds of "nontraditional" principal residence mortgage loans originated after January 1, 2005. Such loans include those that permit the borrower to defer payment of principal or interest or negative amortization of the loan balance, or that have a high-interest "rate spread" as defined by the state law.[48]

4.13 Bankruptcy

Federal bankruptcy laws are intended to enable individuals and their businesses to get fresh starts by temporarily halting collection actions against them and affording them an opportunity to restructure their financial affairs. Contrary to the misimpression some have, bankruptcy does not

---

45. G.S. 1-339.1 through .40.
46. G.S. 45-21.36.
47. G.S. 45-21.38.
48. G.S. 45-21.38A. Rate spread home loans are defined in G.S. 24-1.1F.

simply wipe out debts. In many cases the debtor reorganizes problematic loans and agrees to pay all or most of them according to a new schedule. As the U.S. Supreme Court said, bankruptcy law "gives to the honest but unfortunate debtor . . . a new opportunity in life and a clear field for future effort, unhampered by the pressure and discouragement of preexisting debt."[49]

Federal bankruptcy courts are available in all states. Cases come before specialized bankruptcy judges, and most cases are handled by lawyers who specialize in bankruptcy. The U.S. Trustee Program is a component of the Department of Justice. The office monitors bankruptcy cases and the trustees who are appointed to supervise the collection and distribution of assets in a case.

A bankruptcy filing does not terminate a deed of trust. The rights that a creditor has in real estate before a bankruptcy are constitutionally protected. The creditor is protected to the extent that the loan is secured by value in the debtor's real estate. This is called a *secured claim* in bankruptcy. If the real estate subject to the deed of trust is worth less than the loan, the creditor is considered to be secured for the amount of the real estate's value and unsecured for the rest. Unsecured claims are not constitutionally protected in the same way as secured claims, and in many cases they can be discharged in bankruptcy with partial or no payment.

Most debtors with residential real estate, as well as many other real estate owners, keep their real estate and pay the existing loans that are secured by deeds of trust, often according to a new schedule of payment. In some cases the debtor *liquidates*, receiving a *discharge* from debts in exchange for distributing real estate and other assets to creditors according to a priority and sharing formula. This result has long-term consequences. Lenders will consider someone's recent bankruptcy filing when making lending decisions. But successful completion of a bankruptcy can be a better opportunity to reestablish sound finances than continuing to struggle with nonpayment and creditor collection actions.

4.13.1 Automatic Stay

An important tool available in bankruptcy is a freeze on collection actions. When someone files a petition in federal bankruptcy court, an *automatic stay* prohibits lenders and other creditors from filing or continuing legal

---

49. Local Loan Co. v. Hunt, 292 U.S. 234, 244 (1934).

action against the bankruptcy debtor to collect what is owed. The stay goes into effect immediately when the petition for bankruptcy is filed. But as noted above, a lender who has a secured claim does not lose that right in bankruptcy. The lender's rights to the security are protected, and the court will allow the foreclosure to proceed if the loan is in default and the owner has no equity in the real estate. This is accomplished with a *motion to lift the stay*, by which the creditor requests court approval to continue with the foreclosure sale. The sale will be allowed unless the debtor can cure the default and make future payments.

An additional consideration in bankruptcy reorganization is the concept of *adequate protection*. To protect a secured creditor's property interest while a bankruptcy is pending against accruing debt or diminishing real estate value, the court may order a variety of actions during the bankruptcy. These may include periodic cash payments or a lien on additional property.

A special rule applies to debtors whose only asset is real estate other than a residence. Under certain circumstances a creditor with a claim secured by such real estate may get relief from the stay on an accelerated basis, unless the debtor files a feasible reorganization or begins making interest payments within ninety days of filing or thirty days of the court's determination that the case is a single-asset real estate case.

4.13.2 Bankruptcy Actions and Relief

There are several types of bankruptcy actions under Title 11 of the U.S. Code (known as the Bankruptcy Code), and each is referred to by the chapter of the code that governs it. The most common involving real estate are Chapters 7, 11, 13, and 12.

Chapter 7 is liquidation. In this procedure a court-appointed trustee collects the debtor's assets, sells property, and distributes what is left to creditors. The debtor who is liquidating may retain only very limited property that is exempt, up to a certain amount in a residence and motor vehicle. Often unsecured creditors receive nothing in a liquidation, and the debtor's obligations are discharged with no continuing personal liability for them. The Bankruptcy Code limits Chapter 7 liquidations for individuals only to consumers who have less than a certain amount of income.

Chapter 11 is for reorganization of companies that seek to continue to operate their businesses. It is also available for individuals and must be used by individuals whose income is above a certain amount, but

Chapter 13 has several important advantages for individuals who qualify. Debtors in Chapter 11 must file and obtain court approval of a plan of reorganization, which usually is the product of extensive negotiations with creditors. The plan typically allows the debtor to discharge some of its unsecured obligations, and the law gives some power to terminate contracts. The plan usually involves consolidation and debt reduction.

Chapter 13 is sometimes called *consumer bankruptcy*. It enables the debtor to propose a repayment plan for a set period, usually between three and five years, and to keep some property, such as a house. The debtor must complete the payment plan before the discharge is received. A Chapter 13 bankruptcy filing enables a homeowner with regular income to develop a plan to repay all or part of debts. But to prevent foreclosure on a home for which the loan is in default, a debtor must bring mortgage loans current by paying arrears and commit to make future scheduled payments. If a home is subject to a second mortgage and the real estate value is not sufficient to pay even the first mortgage, the debtor may be able to treat the second mortgage as unsecured debt and obtain approval of a plan that does not require that most or all of it be paid back.

Chapter 12 is for family farmers and family fishermen, and allows them to continue to operate their business while the plan is being carried out. In this procedure, the debtor must have a plan for the repayment of debts over a period of no longer than three years, unless the court approves a longer period not exceeding five years.

Subject Index

Note: Boldface numbers indicate the primary discussion of a topic.